DATE DUE

APR 1 2 2001	
NOV 2 6 2001	
APR 2 1 2007	
~~WITHDRAWN~~	

GAYLORD   #3523PI   Printed in USA

Research, Comparisons and Medical Applications of Ericksonian Techniques

Ericksonian Monographs

Editor

Stephen R. Lankton, M.S.W.

Associate Editors

Research, Comparisons and Medical Applications of Ericksonian Techniques

Edited by Stephen R. Lankton
and Jeffrey K. Zeig

Brunner/Mazel Publishers   •   New York

LIBRARY OF CONGRESS
Library of Congress Cataloging-in-Publication Data

Research, comparisons, and medical applications of Ericksonian
  techniques / edited by Stephen R. Lankton and Jeffrey K. Zeig.
       p.   cm. — (Ericksonian monographs : no. 4)
  Includes bibliographies.
  ISBN 0-87630-510-9
  1. Erickson, Milton H.   2. Hypnotism—Therapeutic use.
  3. Psychotherapy.   I. Lankton, Stephen R.   II. Zeig, Jeffrey K.,
  1947-   . III. Series.
      [DNLM: 1. Erickson, Milton H. 2. Hypnosis. 3. Psychotherapy—
  methods. 4. .Suggestion.   W1 ER44 no. 4 / WM 415 R432.]
  RC495.R47 1988
  615.8'512 — dc 19
  DNLM/DLC
  for Library of Congress
                                                          88-2896
                                                          CIP

Copyright © 1988 by The Milton H. Erickson Foundation

Published by
BRUNNER/MAZEL, INC.
19 Union Square
New York, NY 10003

MANUFACTURED IN THE UNITED STATES OF AMERICA

10 9 8 7 6 5 4 3 2 1

Ericksonian Monographs

Ericksonian Monographs publishes only original manuscripts dealing with Ericksonian approaches to hypnosis, family therapy, and psychotherapy, including techniques, case studies, research and theory.

The *Monographs* will publish only those articles of highest quality that foster the growth and development of the Ericksonian approach and exemplify an original contribution to the fields of physical and mental health. In keeping with the purpose of the *Monographs*, articles should be prepared so that they are readable to a heterogeneous audience of professionals in psychology, medicine, social work, dentistry and related clinical fields.

Publication of the *Ericksonian Monographs* shall be on an irregular basis; no more than three times per year. The Monographs are a numbered, periodical publication. Dates of publication are determined by the quantity of high quality articles accepted by the Editorial Board and the Board of Directors of the Milton H. Erickson Foundation, Inc., rather than calendar dates.

Manuscripts should be *submitted in quintuplicate* (5 copies) with a 100–150-word abstract to Stephen R. Lankton, M.S.W., P.O. Box 958, Gulf Breeze, Florida 32561-0958. Manuscripts of length ranging from 15 to 100 typed double-spaced pages will be considered for publication. Submitted manuscripts cannot be returned to authors. Authors with telecommunication capability may presubmit one copy electronically in either 1200 or 300 baud rate and the following communication parameters: 8 bit word size, No parity, 1 stop bit, x-on/x-off enabled, ASCII and xmodem transfer protocols are acceptable. Call (904) 932-6819 to arrange transmission and security passwords.

Style and format of submitted manuscripts must adhere to instructions described in the *Publication Manual of the American Psychological Association* (3rd edition, 1983). The manuscripts will be returned for revision if reference citations, preparation of tables and figures, manuscript format, avoidance of sexist language, copyright permission for cited material, title page style, etc. do not conform to the *Manual*.

Copyright ownership must be transferred to the Milton H. Erickson Foundation, Inc., if your manuscript is accepted for publication. The Editor's acceptance letter will include a form explaining copyright release, ownership and privileges.

Reference citations should be scrutinized with special care to credit originality and avoid plagiarism. Referenced material should be carefully checked by the author prior to first submission of the manuscript.

Charts and photographs accompanying the manuscripts must be presented in camera-ready form.

Copy editing and galley proofs will be sent to the authors for revisions. Manuscripts must be submitted in clearly written, acceptable, scholarly English. Neither the Editor nor the Publisher is responsible for correcting errors of spelling and grammar: the manuscript, after acceptance, should be immediately ready for publication. Authors should understand there will be a charge passed on to them by the Publisher for revision of galleys.

Prescreening and review procedures for articles is outlined below. Priority is given to those articles which conform to the designated theme for the upcoming *Monographs*. All manuscripts will be prescreened, absented of the author's name, by the Editor or one member of the Editorial Board and one member of either the Continuing Medical Education Committee or the Board of Directors of the Milton H. Erickson Foundation, Inc.

Final acceptance of all articles is done at the discretion of the Board of Directors of the Milton H. Erickson Foundation, Inc. Their decisions will be made after acceptable prescreened articles have been reviewed and edited by a minimum of four persons: two Editorial Board members, one member of the CME Committee or the Board of Directors, and the Editor. Occasionally, reviewers selected by the Editor will assist in compiling feedback to authors.

Feedback for authors and manuscript revision will be handled by the Editor usually between one and two months after submission of the prepared manuscript. Additional inquiries are welcomed if addressed to the Editor.

Contents

Articles

Research

Comparisons

Medical Applications

Contributors

John M. Atthowe, Jr., Ph.D.
University of Medicine and Dentistry-Community Mental Health
Center, Rutgers Medical School, Piscataway, New Jersey

Juliet Auer, C.Q.S.W., M. Phil.
Social worker and psychosexual counselor, Renal Unit, Churchill
Hospital, Oxford, England

Bob Britchford, LRCP, MRCS, MRCPsych
General Practitioner and Consultant Child Psychiatrist in Swindon,
Wiltshire, England

Adam Darnel, M.D.
Department of Psychology, Hebrew University of Jerusalem, Israel

Jeffrey B. Feldman, Ph.D.
Private practice in New York City; Administrative Vice President,
New York Milton H. Erickson Society for Psychotherapy and Hypnosis

Jean Godin, M.D., Ph.D.
Director, Milton H. Erickson Institute of Paris

Steven Goldsmith, M.D.
Attending Physician, Department of Psychiatry, Burbank Hospital,
Fitchburg, Massachusetts; Clinical Instructor in Psychiatry, Boston
University School of Medicine

Lynn Holland, M.S.W.
University of Medicine and Dentistry-Community Mental Health
Center, Rutgers Medical School, Piscataway, New Jersey

Harriet E. Hollander, Ph.D.
Chief Psychologist of Youth Services, University of Medicine and
Dentistry of New Jersey-Community Mental Health Center, Rutgers
Medical School, Piscataway, New Jersey

Michael B. Murphy, M.Phil.
Registered Psychologist in private practice, Auckland, New Zealand

Haim Omer, Ph.D.
Instructor of Psychology, Hebrew University of Jerusalem, Israel

Tzvi Palti, M.D.
Department of Psychology, Hebrew University of Jerusalem, Israel

Maggie Phillips, Ph.D.
Instructor, California Institute of Clinical Hypnosis, and in private
practice and consultation in Oakland, California

Daphna Shuval, M.A.
Department of Psychology, Hebrew University of Jerusalem, Israel

Nehama Silberman, M.A.
Department of Psychology, Hebrew University of Jerusalem, Israel

Introduction

Previous volumes of the Ericksonian Monographs have demonstrated that the effective but sometimes baffling work done in the shadow of Milton H. Erickson's influence can be replicated. Most often Erickson's work is used in hypnotherapy by therapists who, in one way or another, dedicate their practice to his approach. Some professionals who do not designate themselves as Ericksonians may feel his material is out of reach. However, many practitioners are currently discovering Ericksonian principles to be applicable to numerous aspects of therapeutic practice. Three notable areas come to mind, and these are the subject of this volume.

These are three extremely important areas of development in Ericksonian work: research, integration within the practice of other therapies, and medical practice. With this special issue, as with Ericksonian Monographs No. 3, I have again shared editorship with Jeffrey K. Zeig. We bring another invaluable glimpse from the 1986 Third International Congress on Ericksonian Approaches to Hypnosis and Psychotherapy. In so doing we believe the Monographs can further Erickson's influence in these important areas.

Research

The first section of this volume presents research papers from the Third International Congress. These papers are indicative of the wide range of research models attempting to illuminate Erickson's work. Two chapters address the use of indirect suggestion: Jean Godin's "Evocation and Indirect Suggestion in the Communication Patterns of Milton H. Erickson" and Michael B. Murphy's "A Linguistic-Structural Model for the Investigation of Indirect Suggestion." They are among the few attempts to quantify the use of indirect suggestion. In "The Use of Hypnotic-Relaxation Cassettes in a Gynecologic-Obstetric Ward" by Haim Omer, Adam Darnel, Nehama Silberman, Daphna Shuval, and Tzvi Palti, the usefulness of a standardized cassette, while possibly seen as inconsistent with Erickson's work, is handled in a manner of which Erickson would probably have approved. Finally, in this section, a chapter by Harriet E. Hollander, Lynn Holland, and John M. Atthowe, Jr., "Hypnosis: Innate Ability or Learned Skills?" offers data taken from seminar participants to examine this question and draws significant conclusions. The next two sections also consist of manuscripts from the 1986 Ericksonian Congress.

Comparisons

Many therapists appreciate Erickson's work but have established another successful style of work, which they do not wish to abandon. For these therapists, two chapters examine integration by means of comparison and contrast. The first is "The Utilization of Cognition in Psychotherapy: A Comparison of Ericksonian and Cognitive Therapies," by Jeffrey B. Feldman. In the second, "Changing Early Life Decisions Using Ericksonian Hypnosis," Maggie Phillips compares Erickson's approach with that of the Transactional Analysts, Robert and Mary Goulding, and shows how Erickson's approach may be used to enhance the Gouldings' redecision therapy.

Medical Applications

The medical profession often views the use of hypnotic-related therapy as too time consuming to implement within its busy and sometimes chaotic environment. The chapters in this section make it clear that the environmental limitations need not be prohibitive. In "The Application of Ericksonian Principles to the Use of Medication," Steven Goldsmith provides practical techniques for dealing with the problem of getting patients to follow advice on taking medication. Juliet Auer, in "Ericksonian Hypnosis and Psychotherapy in Clinical Settings," illustrates how she improved her functioning in a crowded and crisis-filled emergency room. Bob Britchford wrote the "Ten-Minute Trance: Ericksonian Techniques in a Busy General Medical Practice" to demonstrate that even when only a few minutes are available, useful therapeutic work can be accomplished.

With this issue, we offer an exciting complement to Ericksonian Monographs No. 3. Together, these two volumes illustrate current thinking in important areas of the practice of Ericksonian therapy. They address pragmatic issues confronting professionals who strive to conduct and research Ericksonian therapy.

Stephen R. Lankton
Gulf Breeze, FL
June 1987

Research

Evocation and Indirect Suggestion in the Communication Patterns of Milton H. Erickson

Jean Godin, M.D., Ph.D.

Jean Godin, M.D., Ph.D., is Director of The Milton H. Erickson Institute of Paris. He is co-author of Milton H. Erickson: De l'Hypnose Clinique à la Therapie Strategique, *which is the first book on Erickson originally published in French.*

Godin provides an intriguing schema to analyze indirect suggestions. Subsequently he creates a field study and applies his schema to a portion of one of Erickson's induction transcripts. He illustrates the frequency of several elements in indirect suggestion.

Suggestion is an implicit part of all human interaction and cannot be eliminated from hypnosis or psychotherapy. The present investigation considers suggestion, both direct and indirect, as it is used in hypnosis. The concept and technique of indirect suggestion has been allied with the work of Milton H. Erickson as he used it to replace direct suggestion. A classification system is outlined which articulates the structure and components of direct and indirect suggestions. Using this classification system a hypnotic induction by Milton Erickson is analyzed and several intriguing questions are raised regarding the form and use of suggestions.

Direct Suggestion

What is direct suggestion? During Bernheim's career (Bernheim, 1902), hypnosis was equated with suggestion. At that time, suggestion was an affirmation. In the early practice of hypnosis it was thought sufficient to deliver an affirmation with assurance so that the hypnotic subject would go into a trance. As a result, the subject was then considered to be in a state of readiness to receive other affirmations.

Address reprint requests to Jean Godin, M.D., Ph.D., 28 rue des Écoles, 75005 Paris, France.

While there were failures, many subjects did respond to this approach of induction and suggestion delivery. But this approach was only possible if certain conditions were fulfilled.

Nature and Psychological Impact

The suggestions used in Freud's time were direct suggestions. A series of statements were used which conveyed the information, "That is true because I am telling you so." In such a situation, what can the relationship be between the subject and the omnipotent hypnotist? A great deal has been written on this topic. The consensus in some circles is that a "massive transference" or "psychological regression" occurs.

The myth about hypnosis shared by therapists and patients concerned the power one person can exert over another. This myth, in itself, created a social atmosphere which magnified the suggestive power of statements made by the therapists. The suggestions made by a traditional hypnotist and by Erickson do not have the same psychological impact on the listener. In the traditional case, a patient might understand that the therapist is the origin of a hand levitation or other phenomenon. That is to say, "I (the therapist) have brought it about because I wish to do so, and you are a subject in my hands." In Erickson's approach, the subject is informed in various ways that any phenomena that occur are a function or result of what is happening in the subject's own mind; the therapist's role is minimized. Hypnosis is an exercise which explores certain resources. The therapist can have the status of a "teacher," yet such status should not hinder an egalitarian relationship.

The early writings on the nature of hypnosis, and in particular the writings of Freud, appear to us not to relate to Ericksonian hypnosis. Actually, this relationship imbalance between the hypnotist and subject is nothing but an artifact. It is no more a component of hypnosis than were the hysterical convulsive attacks which were at one time considered an inherent part of the phenomenon.

This chapter provides an analysis of Erickson's suggestion. It reveals that he also used traditional or direct suggestions, but he used them to a much lesser extent.

Indirect Suggestion

Erickson's approach defines hypnosis as a state of heightened inner concentration where attention is concerned with one's memories, values, thoughts, and beliefs about life. We can assume that the hypnotic state is nothing more than entering into one's own "self" so that unconscious phenomena appear in the foreground due to a temporary dissociation from the realities of the surrounding world. We can be thankful to Erickson for demonstrating that there are other means to obtain a hypnotic state beside direct suggestion. One such technique is indirect suggestion.

While Milton Erickson did not invent indirect suggestion, he did emphasize its importance. However, one may still ask, "What is an indirect suggestion?" Milton Erickson had little interest in theorizing; he did not always distinguish between and delineate the characteristics of the suggestions he used. One might expect these characteristics to be uniform, but this does not appear to be the case. The present work analyzes suggestion along five polar parameters. This leads to a classification of suggestions along the following five polarities: 1) evocation versus compliance-based suggestion (referred to as suggestion, for short); 2) visible versus invisible perception of suggestion; 3) authoritarian versus permissive suggestions; 4) obligation versus freedom in response; and 5) conscious versus unconscious mediation. Each of these will be examined briefly before being applied to a transcript that represents a well-known case treated successfully by Erickson.

Classification of Suggestions

Purpose: External Suggestion or Evocation

The primary and perhaps most important differences between traditional and Ericksonian approaches are the concepts of external suggestion versus evocation. For Bernheim, suggestion was imposing an idea upon another person who must submit to the idea. For Erickson, suggestion was a tool for evocation or elicitation of an existing unconscious possibility or potential from the subject. These are radically different purposes.

Whether it is the hypnotic phenomenon, a specific hypnotic phenomenon, or a therapeutic possibility, for Erickson nothing could appear which had not previously existed in the subject. Therefore, the problem for him was not to "suggest" a compliance but to "evoke" a potential.

For Erickson, internal responses represented the indirect aspect of hypnotic communication: "You make a lot of statements to patients that evoke certain *natural associative responses* within them. It is these responses *within them* that are the essence of hypnotic suggestion" (Erickson & Rossi, 1981, p. 28). As Rossi notes, hypnosis is the facilitation of a process in which the subjects give suggestions to themselves (Erickson et al., 1976). Thus, suggestion is not blind acceptance or obedience, but a "response."

There is, at a certain level, a self-dialogue: "Do I want to or not?" This dialogue is not addressed to the superficial level of the conscious mind, it is addressed to the subject's unconscious, which perhaps is not aware of what the subject wants consciously.

This is why trance does not assure acceptance of suggestions. It is a modality in which the mental processes of the subject have an opportunity to interact in a spontaneous and autonomous way with the hypnotist. This new, Ericksonian approach, based on evocation, has nothing in common with traditional and/or classical suggestion and, actually, should be referred to with a different term.

Subject's Perception of the Suggestion

An indirect suggestion can be said to be a suggestion the subject's conscious mind cannot perceive. Many of the statements used by Erickson are, in this sense, *invisible*. For Erickson, this characteristic is of major importance. In fact, if the subject understands that something is being asked, it is difficult to distinguish what aspect of the subject's response is voluntary and what is not. If the subject is not aware of what has been asked by the suggestion, the subject's associated response will always contain an element of surprise. As mentioned, this creates a true hypnotic response. Suggestions which are intended to result in very obvious responses will be called *visible*.

Degree of Direction of the Suggestion

Since the suggestions of traditional hypnosis are authoritarian, the hypnotic response is confused with obedience. The authoritarian approach can be exemplified by the use of the linguistic imperative, "Sleep!" or the present indicative, "Your eyes are closing," or the future tense, "I am going to count to 5." These subtleties of language have, for ths study, the same value. As mentioned, they imply that the hypnotist has an *authoritarian* role to which the subject must comply.

Permissiveness is generally a part of Erickson's approach. The linguistic structure might be, "Sooner or later your eyes might close." In this approach, the social and psychological relationship between the hypnotist and subject is quite different. Such suggestions will be classified as *permissive*.

Degree of Freedom in Response to the Suggestion

In the case of permissive versus authoritarian suggestions, the major concern is the subject's interpretation of the suggestion. Here, the question is the degree of real constraint. For example, the evocation of a phenomenon tends to bring about its realization by ideomotor effect. This type of suggestion, then, would be rated as *obligation*.

Mediation of the Suggestion

For Erickson a response merits the label "hypnotic" if it is mediated at an unconscious level. This process appears to be involuntary. If one directs a subject to close his or her eyes, it is normal to think that the response is voluntary because the subject accommodates with *conscious* mediation. By contrast, if the evocation of the sensation of sun on the skin produces a vasodilation or anesthesia, the phenomenon is mediated at an *unconscious* level.

Classification of Ericksonian Suggestion

While many other characteristics can describe suggestions, the above are of primary importance for practitioners. A "purely" indirect suggestion could be described as evocative, invisible, permissive, free in reference to response, and mediated unconsciously. A detailed analysis may show that not all the specific means of communication employed by Erickson have all these five characteristics. The classification system will enable us to discern which combination of elements are contained in each statement.

Summary of the Classification System

A suggestion can be characterized on the above five variables. A statement can be an evocation (E) or a compliance-based suggestion (S) according to whether the phenomenon is perceived as being part of the potential inherent in the subject or external to the subject (namely, in the therapist). A statement will be either invisible (I) or visible (V) to the subject. A statement will be experienced as permissive (P) or authoritarian (A). A statement will allow the subject freedom (F) or will tend to create an obligation (O). A statement will tend to be mediated by the unconscious (U) or be presented as if only the conscious (C) is concerned. Thus, an indirect statement or suggestion could be codified as E I P F U; whereas, a direct suggestion could be codified as S V A O C. This classification system is delineated in Table 1.

Analysis of an Erickson Transcript

To apply this classification to Erickson's suggestions, a well-known training tape, for which a written transcript exists, "The Artistry of Milton

Table 1

Characteristics of Suggestions

Suggestion (S)	Visible (V)	Authoritarian (A)	Obligation (O)	Conscious (C)
Evocation (E)	Invisible (I)	Permissive (P)	Freedom (F)	Unconscious (U)

H. Erickson, M.D." (Lustig, 1975), was used. Fifty statements by Erickson were chosen for the analysis, as they appear to be a representative sample. Each suggestion was categorized according to the above dimensions. The results are summarized below.

Seventy percent (70%) of the total statements were evocations and 30% were compliance-based suggestions. Fifty percent (50%) of the statements were visible and 50% were invisible. Eighty percent (80%) of the statements were permissive and 20% were authoritarian. Fifty percent (50%) of the statements attempted to lead the patient unconsciously in a desired direction. Eighty percent (80%) of the statements used unconscious mediation and 20% used conscious mediation. Of the 50 statements, 3 (5%) were E I P F U; 17 (34%) were E I P O U; and the remaining 30 were comprised of a variety of possible combinations, for example, E V P F U, E V P F C, S V A F C, S V A D U, and S V A O C.

Conclusion

An analysis of two different forms of suggestion used in the practice of hypnosis, with specific attention to the indirect techniques of Milton H. Erickson, was presented. Suggestions were characterized on five dimensions: reference source, perception, direction, freedom of response, and level of mediation. These characteristics were determined by asking: Is it an evocation or a compliance-based suggestion? Is the aim discernible to the subject? Is the statement permissive? Does the statement exercise a certain constraint on the psyche of the subject? Is the suggestion mediated at an unconscious level?

Milton Erickson's approach to hypnosis makes extensive use of a psychological orientation that may be termed "evocation." This procedure is, by its nature, very different from compliance-based suggestion. It does not aim to impose an idea upon the subject but to elicit the potentials that are assumed to exist within the subject. This establishes a different quality of relationship between the hypnotist and the subject.

Through studying one of Dr. Erickson's inductions, it was found that his statements can have the various qualities described in this paper. However, rarely does each suggestion or statement have all five characteristics. This analysis suggests that in order to consider a suggestion as indirect, it must possess at least two or more of these five characteristics. Since the major interest of this chapter was to elaborate a working tool to compare different forms of suggestion, this work must be considered exploratory.

References

Bernheim, H. (1902). *Suggestive therapeutics*. New York: Putnam.

Erickson, M. H., Rossi, E. L., & Rossi, S. I. (1976). *Hypnotic realities: The induction of clinical hypnosis and forms of indirect suggestion*. New York: Irvington.

Erickson, M. H., & Rossi, E. L. (1980). The indirect forms of suggestion. In E. L. Rossi (Ed.), *The collected papers of Milton H. Erickson on hypnosis: Vol. 1. The nature of hypnosis and suggestion* (pp. 452–477). New York: Irvington.

Erickson, M. H., & Rossi, E. L. (1981). *Experiencing hypnosis: Therapeutic approaches to altered states*. New York: Irvington.

Lustig, H. (1975). *The artistry of Milton H. Erickson, M.D., Part I and Part II* (a video tape). Haverford, PA: Herbert S. Lustig, M.D., Ltd.

A Linguistic-Structural Model for the Investigation of Indirect Suggestion

Michael B. Murphy, M.Phil.

Michael B. Murphy, M.Phil., was born and educated in New Zealand. In New Zealand he has presented workshops in Ericksonian methods, and in the counseling and case management of intrafamilial child sexual abuse.

Murphy's study is one of the few existent attempts to systematize and measure the effects of indirect suggestion. He began by simplifying the variety of Ericksonian indirect suggestions to two main subtypes. In a nonhypnotic setting, he compared the effect of those subtypes to direct suggestion. His study offers an alternative schema of classification which, as he puts it, may prove useful as "A Linguistic-Structural Model for the Investigation of Indirect Suggestion."

Milton Erickson's contribution to the therapeutic use of hypnosis and suggestion was characterized by the "utilization approach" (Erickson, 1959) and by the use of indirect forms of suggestion (Erickson & Rossi, 1979, 1980). Erickson and Rossi (1980) assert that "indirect suggestion tends to bypass conscious criticism and because of this can be more effective than direct suggestion" (p. 455). The absence of empirical support for this assertion prompted me to embark upon an experiment that would investigate whether indirect suggestion is in fact more effective than direct suggestion.

This chapter reviews the simplified linguistic-structural model developed for the standardizing of suggestion forms, and the initial experimental investigation of the effectiveness of some simple forms of direct and indirect suggestion (Murphy, 1985). Since it was decided to investigate suggestion per se in a nonhypnotic, nonclinical setting, the effects that controlling hypnotic and clinical variables may have had are discussed. Directions for further research are also considered.

Address reprint requests to Michael B. Murphy, M.Phil., 43 O'Neill Street, Auckland, New Zealand 1002.

A Linguistic-Structural Model

The task of selecting forms of indirect suggestion that can be standardized for experimental study was begun by reviewing analyses of Erickson's use of suggestion. Most are similar to Erickson and Rossi's (1980) analysis, which lists 12 major categories of indirect suggestion:

1. Indirect Associative Focusing
2. Truisms Utilizing Ideodynamic Processes and Time
3. Questions That Focus, Suggest and Reinforce
4. Implication
5. Therapeutic Binds and Double Binds
6. Compound Suggestions: Yes Set, Reinforcement, Shock, and Surprise
7. Contingent Associations and Associational Networks
8. The Implied Directive
9. Open-Ended Suggestions
10. Covering All Possibilities of Response
11. Apposition of Opposites
12. Dissociation and Cognitive Overloading (p. 456)

Bandler and Grinder (1975) propose a linguistic analysis of Erickson's use of suggestion which includes five major categories of linguistic structures: Linguistic Causal Modeling Processes, Transderivational Search Phenomena, Ambiguities, Lesser Included Structures, and Derived Meanings.

In both analyses most forms described and illustrated are quite complex; however, two relatively simple indirect forms are apparent. I have termed these *truisms* and *presuppositions*. Since the experiment conducted (Murphy, 1985) compared the effectiveness of these two simple indirect forms with that of simple direct suggestion, truisms, presuppositions, and direct suggestions are defined and illustrated below.

Truisms

Erickson and Rossi (1980) define a truism as "a simple statement of fact about behavior" (p. 457), and give examples such as "Everyone has had the experience of nodding their head" (p. 457). Bandler and Grinder (1975) describe truistic statements in their discussion of noun phrases with "generalized referential index" (p. 157), a subcategory of transderivational search phenomena. They give examples such as "People can be comfortable while reading this sentence" (p. 157).

Presuppositions

Bandler and Grinder (1975) describe presuppositions as a subset of the class of linguistic constructions, Derived Meanings. "The formal representation of what constitutes presuppositions in natural language is as follows: Message A is a presupposition of Message B when Message A must be a true statement necessary for both message B and the message Not B" (p. 242).

The statement "I know when you will close your eyes" is an example of this statement form, in which it is presupposed that the listener will close his or her eyes. The statement "I don't know when you will close your eyes" also presupposes the same response.

The remaining subset of the class Derived Meanings is Conversational Postulates. These are also statements which presuppose a certain response on the part of the listener and hence may be regarded as presuppositions. Examples given include "Can you open the door?" (p. 243) and "You may go now" (p. 244).

Covering all possibilities of response and *therapeutic binds and double binds*, two of Erickson and Rossi's (1980) categories of indirect suggestion, seem to consist of presuppositions. Examples given include "Would you like to go into trance now or in a few minutes?" (p. 460) and "You can scribble, or make a mark or a line here or there. You can write a letter here or there. A syllable here a syllable there" (p. 468). In the first example the development of trance is presupposed; in the second, writing behavior of some sort is presupposed.

Direct Suggestions

Direct suggestions have the form of simple commands such as, "Close your eyes," "Let yourself relax," "You are getting sleepy." The class of linguistic constructions, Lesser Included Structures, (Bandler & Grinder, 1975) consists of direct suggestions included within a more complex indirect suggestion form. For example, the sentence "I wonder whether you would like to close your eyes" contains the lesser included direct suggestion "Close your eyes."

Erickson altered his voice tone or the direction of his speech when stating lesser included suggestions, or he paused before and after them in order to give emphasis to the suggestion without the listener being consciously aware of the emphasis thus given. Most of the indirect suggestion forms listed by Bandler and Grinder (1975) and Erickson and Rossi (1980) have potential for the inclusion of direct suggestions in this manner. Hence it is possible to view direct suggestions as structural elements of many indirect forms.

Composite Forms of Indirect Suggestion

The observation that many indirect forms contain lesser included direct suggestions led to the observation that the more complex forms of indirect suggestion are composed of either a truistic statement and a direct suggestion, or a truistic statement and a presupposing suggestion. Hence, linguistic constructions termed *truisms, presuppositions* and *direct suggestions*, as defined above, can be considered to be structural elements from which virtually all indirect suggestion forms can be constructed.

A review of all the indirect suggestion forms listed by Bandler and Grinder (1975) and Erickson and Rossi (1980), other than those subsumed under the simpler truism and presupposition forms, illustrates this assertion.

Composites: Truism-Plus-Direct-Suggestion

Several of the categories of indirect suggestion listed by Erickson and Rossi (1980) can be constructed by combining a truism with a direct suggestion. Often these constructions imply a causative link between the truism and the direct suggestion, although logically no such causation exists.

Implication. "If you sit down, then you can go into trance" (p. 459). In this example, especially if the listener has just sat down, or is about to sit down, the first clause is a truistic statement; "you can go into trance" can be viewed as a direct suggestion.

Implied Directive. "Your right hand will descend to your thigh as soon as you know that only you and I...are here" (p. 466). "Your right hand will descend to your thigh" is a direct suggestion; "you know that only you and I...are here" is a truistic statement. Hence, in this example the order is direct suggestion plus truism.

Contingent Associations. "Your eyes will get tired and close all by themselves as you continue looking at that spot" (p. 464). As in the above example, the order is direct suggestion, then truism.

Apposition of Opposites. "As your hand feels light and lifts, your eyelids will feel heavy and close" (p. 470). In this example, it is possible that Erickson was commenting upon an existing hand levitation, hence using a truism. He has followed it with a direct suggestion for eye closure.

Dissociation and Cognitive Overloading. This category of indirect suggestion is generally used in association with the induction of confusion

(Erickson, 1964). The following example is a complex form in which truisms are presented in an overloading quantity. The direct suggestion is given in the last sentence embedded in an alternative. "You can stand up or sit down. You can sit in that chair or the other. You can go out this door or that. You can come back to see me or refuse to see me. You can get well or remain sick. You can improve or you can get worse. You can accept therapy or you can refuse it. Or you can go into trance to find out what you want" (p. 470).

Bandler and Grinder (1975) describe this composite form in their category Linguistic Causal Modeling, which refers to the pseudocausal link which is implied in these forms of indirect suggestion. They give examples such as "Sitting all the way down in that chair will make you go into a deep trance" (p. 211) and "As you listen to the sound of my voice, you will relax more and more" (p. 212). Both of these examples are constructed from a truistic statement followed by a pseudocausal link to a direct suggestion.

Composites: Truism-Plus-Presupposition

Examples from four of Erickson and Rossi's (1980) categories have the composite form of one or more truisms combined with a presupposition.

Compound Suggestions. Erickson is quoted as having said to one of his daughters when she returned from a visit to an orthodontist, "That mouthful of hardware that you've got in your mouth is miserably uncomfortable and it's going to be a deuce of a job to get used to it" (p. 463). The statements "That mouthful of hardware that you've got in your mouth" and "is miserably uncomfortable" are consistent with the two definitions of truisms given above. The statement "it's going to be a deuce of a job to get used to it" presupposes that Erickson's daughter will get used to the uncomfortable mouthful of hardware.

Open-Ended Suggestions. "Every person has abilities not known to the self.... Yet they are available to the unconscious and can be experienced within trance now or later whenever the unconscious is ready" (p. 468). The statements "Every person has abilities not known to the self" and "Yet they are available to the unconscious" are truistic statements, provided one accepts Erickson's implicit theory regarding an unconscious mind and a self. The remainder of the quotation is a truistic bind which presupposes that a person can experience unconscious abilities in trance.

Questions That Focus, Suggest and Reinforce. The following question presupposes tiredness as the meaning of subsequent blinking. "As you continue looking at that spot, do your eyes get tired and have a tendency to blink?" (p. 458). "As you continue looking at that spot" is a truistic observation about the listener's on-going experience. The subsequent question presupposes eye-tiredness as the meaning of any blinking.

In all of the composite examples listed, the truisms or truistic statements referred to, while consistent with the definitions given, are statements that describe, or "pace" (Bandler & Grinder, 1975, p. 15), an aspect of the listener's on-going experience but are not suggestions per se. Their function in the utilization approach to suggestion (Erickson, 1959) is to elicit an attitude of agreement on the part of the subject, and to distract him or her from the attached suggestion.

In the above review of Erickson and Rossi's (1980) and Bandler and Grinder's (1975) analyses of Erickson's use of indirect suggestion, only Erickson and Rossi's category of *Indirect Associative Focusing* and Bandler and Grinder's *Ambiguities* have not been discussed. Indirect Associative Focusing is a term used to denote Erickson's use of casual conversation, anecdote and metaphor as vehicles for introducing ideas and covert indirect suggestions, and is described by Bandler and Grinder (1975) as a subcategory of Transderivational Search Phenomena. I consider this category of suggestion as providing a rich context for indirect suggestion, rather than as a specific form which can be standardized for experimental investigation.

Bandler and Grinder's (1975) category of Ambiguities usefully describes an aspect of Erickson's use of confusion (Erickson, 1964). Several of the examples given do not contain suggestions, as such, but tend to be ambiguous truisms, such as "They are visiting relatives" (p. 234). However, one example, "I want you to notice your hand me that glass" (p. 236), can be seen to be a composite indirect suggestion composed of a truistic remark about the speaker's wish, "I want you to," followed by two direct suggestions, "notice your hand" and "hand me that glass." The two direct suggestions have been linked by deleting one occurrence of the word "hand," thus creating a punctuation ambiguity. This suggestion has the form of truism plus direct suggestion.

Hence, from the point of view of linguistic-structural composition, all of the forms of suggestion described in both of the analyses I examined can be considered to be truisms, presuppositions, or composites of either truism(s)-plus-direct-suggestion(s), or truism(s)-plus-presupposition(s). This linguistic structural model of indirect suggestions, and its relationship to the two analyses examined, is depicted in Table 1. This simplified structural analysis may provide a model with which standardization of various simple and complex forms of indirect suggestion can be achieved. Such standardization may enable the effectiveness of various indirect forms to be evaluated and, hence, inferences to be made regarding the relative effectiveness of indirect forms in general.

Table 1

Comparison of Three Analyses of Indirect Suggestion

	Bandler & Grinder (1975)	Erickson & Rossi (1980)
Truisms	Generalized Referential Index	Truisms
Presuppositions	Presuppositions Conversational Postulates	Therapeutic Binds Covering All Possibilities
Truism-Plus-Direct-Suggestion	Linguistic Causal Modeling Conversational Postulates Ambiguities	Implication Implied Directive Contingent Associations Apposition of Opposites Dissociation and Cognitive Overloading
Truism-Plus-Presupposition		Compound Suggestions Questions That Focus, Suggest and Reinforce Open-Ended Suggestions

An Initial Investigation

As an initial, exploratory investigation, I designed and conducted an experiment (Murphy, 1985) which evaluated behavioral responsiveness to simple direct suggestion and the two simple forms of indirect suggestion, truism and presupposition. This experiment was seen as a first step in what must necessarily become a much more extensive inquiry, and in that sense it is by no means an adequate test of the relative effectiveness of indirect suggestion in general. It examined only two simple forms of indirect suggestion, drawn from a larger set of more complex forms. Also, many clinical variables were controlled (i.e., by presenting suggestions via audiotape) in an attempt to assess responsiveness to the suggestions per se.

Hypothesis

The experimental hypothesis was derived from Erickson and Rossi's (1980) assertion, "Indirect suggestion...can be more effective than direct suggestion" (p. 455), and is stated: *Indirect suggestions will result in a significantly greater behavioral responsiveness than direct suggestions.*

Measure of Responsiveness

The measure of behavioral responsiveness to suggestion chosen was forward postural movement. Postural sway is a typical example of *primary suggestibility*, the main factor of suggestibility which has consistently emerged from factor analytic studies (As & Lauer, 1962; Eysenck, 1947; Hammer et al., 1963; Moore, 1964). Hull (1933) and Eysenck (1947) extensively used postural sway as a measure of response to suggestion, and it is one of the battery of measures used in the Stanford Hypnotic Susceptibility Scales (SHSS) (Weitzenhofer & Hilgard, 1959). In this investigation postural movement was recorded on video and measurements taken from a calibrated line placed on the video monitor screen.

Experimental Design Conditions

An independent group design was used with four conditions: direct suggestions, truisms, presuppositions, and control (no suggestions). Four magnetic audiotapes were prepared which contained a standardized set of instructions, a 10-second pause, a 30-second set of six suggestions (or control statements), a further 10-second pause, and an instruction that the experimental procedure had finished.

The initial instructions told the subject simply to stand with his or her eyes closed and to listen to the subsequent 30 seconds of recorded "comments."

The direct suggestions were largely borrowed from one of Hull's (1933) experiments in which he used recorded suggestions. The truism, presupposition, and control statements were generated in such a way that the six statements on each tape had an identical sequence of statement and pause duration, thus controlling any effects which may arise from the duration of time of spoken sounds and silence used. The actual recorded suggestions used were as follows.

Direct Suggestions. "During the next few seconds you will tend to fall forward. Now you will begin to feel yourself fall forward. You are beginning to fall forward. You are falling forward. You are falling forward a little more. You fall forward over on to your toes."

Truisms. "People listening to these comments tend to fall forward. Most people will fall forward to some extent. Some fall forward just a little. Others fall forward a lot. Some fall further and further forward. Others fall forward enough to lose their balance."

Presuppositions. "These comments enhance your tendency to fall forward. I don't know just how far you will fall forward. If you will fall forward just a little, or fall forward a lot. Maybe you will be rather slow to fall forward. Perhaps you will fall forward quite quickly."

Control. "Recording onto tapes requires a few choices. Cassette tapes come in a variety of lengths. Two hour tapes are rare now. Short ones are, too. Many people use C90 tapes. This one happens to be a C46."

In each of the three suggestion conditions, the lesser included structure "fall forward" occurs six times, thus standardizing the occurrence of the embedded direct suggestion. As a further control on this variable, five people used a five-point scale to rate the consistency of the tone of voice on the tapes. A mean "similarity" estimate of 84% was obtained where 80% corresponded to *very similar* and 100% corresponded to *completely identical*.

A reliability check on the author's classification of suggestion statements was also conducted. Five people who are familiar with the use of indirect suggestion forms classified the 24 recorded statements from a randomized list, into the categories: direct suggestion, truism, presupposition, none of the above. Agreement with the author's classification was 82.67%, with individual scores ranging from 70.0% to 96.67%. An analysis of the individual scores revealed that two of the classifiers had "correctly" classified the control statements as being truisms. If the control statements are ignored, the mean score for classifying the suggestion forms is 87.78% with a range of individual scores 77.78% to 94.44%.

Subjects and Matching

A total 108 subjects were drawn from undergraduate classes in Education and Psychology at the University of Auckland, New Zealand. There were 72 women and 36 men, reflecting the composition of the students in those departments. Subjects were matched across the four experimental conditions by gender since, although there appear to be no significant gender differences in suggestibility, data is inconsistent (Eysenck, 1947; Hilgard, 1967; Hull, 1933; Weitzenhoffer & Weitzenhoffer, 1958). Matching by age-group was also employed since, although suggestibility appears to be stable after mid-teenage years (Barber & Glass, 1962), Eysenck (1947) suggested a gradual decrease during adult life. Within the groups matched by gender and age, subjects were randomly assigned to the experimental condition.

E. R. Hilgard's (1967) review of research into personality correlates of suggestibility indicates no correlations of suggestibility with intelligence or other traits, although some developmental variables may influence adult suggestibility (Hilgard & Hilgard, 1962). Correlations between childhood fantasy, adult role-taking ability, and suggestibility (J. R. Hilgard, 1970) are supported by Sarbin and Lim's (1963) finding that drama students were more suggestible than physical science students. I assume that the selection of subjects from two similar academic fields provided a relatively homogeneous experimental population which did not include high proportions of either extremes of suggestibility.

Matching by suggestibility scores was rejected since the author wished to examine suggestion per se and avoid the complexities introduced through the use of hypnosis. Defining the situation as hypnosis has been found to influence responsiveness to suggestion (Barber & Calverley, 1964) and the use of either of the popular suggestibility scales could invite such definition. The SHSS utilizes a hypnotic induction procedure and, like the Barber Suggestibility Scale (Barber & Glass, 1962), includes items commonly associated with hypnosis, particularly in its entertainment forms. Further, the SHSS includes the Postural Sway Test, thus introducing a possible practice effect into an investigation in which postural sway was used as the measure of suggestibility.

Data Recorded

Eighteen position data were recorded per subject, during the 50-second period following the initial taped instructions. Four data were taken during the 10-second pause preceding suggestions (or control statements) to provide a baseline measure for each subject. Fourteen further data were recorded during the 30 seconds of spoken statements and the subsequent 10 seconds of silence. Using 72 data from a sample of four subjects, test-retest reliability of 82% and interobserver reliability of 87.5% were obtained. An analysis of the data disagreements indicated two experimental artifacts as the greatest sources of disagreement. Data reliability was considered acceptable.

Measures of Dependent Variable

Since responding was observed to be highly variable across subjects, three measures of response were calculated in order to address different aspects of responding over both distance and duration of postural movement. The subject's greatest forward movement was noted and termed Greatest Sway, the mean position during the final 10 seconds was calculated and termed Final Position, and the mean position over the 40 seconds of suggestions and subsequent silence was termed Mean Position.

Means and standard deviations for each of the three measures, across the experimental conditions, are shown in Table 2. A consistent pattern emerged in the means obtained, being, in order of greatest to least: direct suggestions, presuppositions, truisms, and the control condition. These results challenge the experimental hypothesis.

Table 2

Three Measures of Postural Sway as a Function of Suggestion Condition

| | Measures of Postural Sway (in mm) | | | | | |
| | Greatest | | Final | | Mean | |
Condition	M	SD	M	SD	M	SD
Direct	21.3	25.7	12.2	26.4	6.6	17.4
Presupposition	16.4	16.4	4.8	16.7	4.2	13.6
Truism	11.4	10.5	1.7	12.0	1.1	8.4
Control	8.1	10.7	-2.2	9.2	-1.3	8.6

Results

An omnibus F-test one-way analysis of variance, for the variables Greatest Sway and Final Position, rejects the null hypothesis ($p<0.05$) that data are drawn from the same population. Thus further comparisons with these variables are justified. For Mean Position further comparisons are unjustified as the null hypothesis is accepted ($p=0.18$). For Greatest Sway and Final Position the pooled suggestion conditions are significantly different ($p<0.05$) from the control condition. Thus, suggestions do produce responses.

Since the consistent trend observed in the data indicates results opposite to the experimental hypothesis, further comparisons were treated as unplanned and the conservative Scheffé test employed. This results in acceptance of the null hypothesis ($p<0.05$) that there is no significant difference between direct suggestion and the pooled indirect suggestion conditions. Thus the experimental hypothesis is rejected for the truism and presupposition forms of indirect suggestion.

Discussion

Further Comparisons

Although the experimental hypothesis regarding the relative effectiveness of direct and indirect suggestion was rejected for the two simple forms of indirect suggestion examined, further unplanned statistical comparisons were made. I am particularly interested in the means observed for direct suggestions and presuppositions.

Using the measure Final Position, the Scheffé test indicates that direct suggestion data is significantly different from the data pooled from all other conditions ($p<0.05$), lending support to the alternative hypothesis that direct suggestion was more effective than the indirect forms used for this study.

Using the measure Greatest Sway, the Scheffé test indicates that judgement must be suspended with regard to either rejecting or accepting the hypotheses that: 1) direct suggestions are significantly different from all other conditions pooled; 2) direct suggestions are significantly different from the control group; 3) presuppositions are significantly different from the control group; and 4) direct suggestions and presuppositions pooled are significantly different from truisms and control pooled. These results suggest that both direct suggestions and presuppositions may produce significant behavioral responding whereas truisms may not.

The Complex Forms of Indirect Suggestion

The results of the comparisons described above are of particular interest since all of the complex forms of indirect suggestion reviewed contain either an embedded direct suggestion or a presupposition, linked to a truistic statement. Indeed, most of the examples of the complex forms given contain a direct suggestion concealed with the indirect form. Given the accumulation of possibly significant support for direct suggestion found in this investigation, one aspect of further investigations might well be an experiment which sets out to test the hypothesis that indirect suggestions that include a direct suggestion are more effective than the undisguised direct suggestion itself. Likewise, complex forms which contain a presupposition may be more effective than presuppositions in their simple forms.

A further consideration with regard to the role of direct suggestions as a component of the indirect forms is the use of embedded direct suggestions as lesser included structures within the indirect forms. In this investigation, the voice tone used on the tapes of suggestions was kept constant in order to control this variable. However, in clinical practice Erickson made extensive use of voice tone shifts and pauses to "analogically mark" (Bandler & Grinder, 1975, p. 24) hidden direct suggestions built into his communications. All of the indirect forms have potential for the use of this procedure, and some effectiveness associated with indirect suggestion may thus be attributable to hidden direct suggestions.

The absence of complex forms of indirect suggestion in this investigation seriously limits inferences which can be made regarding the overall hypothesis. A next step in investigation must be to evaluate experimentally the responsiveness produced by some complex forms of indirect suggestion. Since the combinations truism-plus-direct-suggestion and truism-plus-presupposition account for all of the complex forms, two experimental conditions can be created such that each condition consists of suggestions of one construction or the other.

The Utilization Approach

In describing Erickson's therapeutic use of hypnosis and suggestion, Erickson and Rossi (1979) point out that the use of indirect suggestion is an aspect of the utilization approach (Erickson, 1959).

> The utilization approach and the indirect forms of suggestion are the two major means of facilitating these overall dynamics of therapeutic trance and suggestion. The utilization approach emphasizes the continual involvement of each patient's unique repertory of abilities and potentials, while the indirect forms of suggestion are the means by which the therapist facilitates these involvements. (pp. 14–15)

Utilization involves the linking of suggestions to the ongoing behavior or experience of the listener, thus utilizing the behavior or experience in a manner that facilitates the acceptance of the suggestions. All of the complex forms of indirect suggestion are examples of utilization in which a truistic comment about the listener's ongoing behavior or experience is associated with either a direct suggestion or a presupposition.

In this investigation, no complex forms of indirect suggestion were used, and the standardization of the suggestion-giving procedures prevented or randomized the possibility of suggestion statement coinciding with utilizable responses. In fact, a review of the videotaped responding showed that many subjects swayed forward to a small degree after each of several suggestion statements, however these responses were too small and too brief to be represented in the measurements taken. These minimal yet observable responses could well be utilized in a less standardized situation with, for example, a statement such as, "As you fall forward a little you may wonder when you will fall forward a lot." The clinical application of the utilization approach often involves the repeated linking of small responses to suggestions that greater, or perhaps similar, more clinically relevant responses will follow.

Utilization has been investigated experimentally by Barber and DeMoor (1972) in conjunction with direct suggestion forms. The combining of suggestions with naturally occurring events was found to augment responsiveness to test suggestions. Since this type of utilization would seem more readily available with the use of complex indirect suggestions than with direct, the incorporation of the utilization variable may enhance responsiveness to indirect suggestion more than direct.

Erickson and Rossi (1980) speculated about the role that utilization may have in the effective use of indirect suggestion.

> Experimental research will be needed to establish the comparative merit of direct and indirect suggestion while controlling subject, operator, and response variables.... These indirect forms are also frequently used in association with his utilization approach (Erickson, 1959), wherein he uses the subject's own behaviour to enhance the development of hypnotic responses. Because of this the junior author would hypothesize that in factoral experimental designs the interaction of *indirect approaches x utilization* would be more significant than the main effect of either factor alone. (p. 475)

The results of this investigation indicate that simple indirect suggestion forms used *in the absence of utilization procedures* do not produce greater behavioral responses than direct suggestions. The introduction of utilization procedures is a necessary step in further investigation.

The Clinical Setting

In this investigation, variables which can be active in the clinical setting were controlled. In particular, the experimental procedure was designed to minimize expectations that the subjects might have regarding the specific nature of the responses measured, and the response of forward postural sway is unlikely to have relevance to the subject's personal situation.

People who consult a clinician for assistance with a personal situation have some degree of expectancy that personally relevant results will follow. The clinical setting itself is a form of indirect suggestion that useful results will occur. Erickson's work was almost entirely clinical and his reputation for extraordinary effectiveness engendered high level of expectancy in his patients. His assertion regarding the effectiveness of indirect suggestion was made in this context of high expectations of personally relevant results.

Experimentally, the variable of expectancy of responsiveness has been shown to augment responding (Barber & Calverley, 1963; Melei & Hilgard, 1964). The control of this variable in this investigation may have contributed to the attenuated responsiveness observed, and its systematic introduction into further experimentation is necessary in order to assess its contribution to the responsiveness Erickson asserted for indirect suggestion in the clinical setting.

Summary

A review of two analyses of Milton H. Erickson's use of indirect verbal suggestion led to a simplified linguistic analysis in which structural elements of indirect suggestion were isolated. These elemental forms of suggestion comprise the suggestion conditions employed in an initial investigation and provide a model for further investigation, particularly of the complex indirect suggestion forms which are combinations of these elements.

This limited investigation cannot be considered an adequate test of the effectiveness of indirect suggestion in general. However, it may provide a model for further multifactoral investigations.

Of particular interest are the results that indicate that data for both direct suggestions and presuppositions approached significance. Since both direct suggestion and presupposition elements occur in all complex indirect suggestion structures, an investigation of the complex forms may find them to be more effective than their constituent elements. That most complex forms contain an embedded direct suggestion, the form that produced consistent, near-significant results in this investigation, is further support for this conjecture.

The complex forms of indirect suggestion are also closely related to Erickson's utilization approach to the clinical use of suggestion. The initial investigation of the basic indirect forms was designed to control utilization effects and to examine responsiveness produced by the basic forms in and of themselves. In order to fully explore the implication of Erickson's assertion regarding the effectiveness of indirect suggestion, further investigation is necessary using the complex forms and incorporating the variables of utilization and contextual influence.

References

As, A., & Lauer, L. W. (1962). A factor analytic study of hypnotizability and related personal experiences. *International Journal of Clinical and Experimental Hypnosis, 10*(3), 169–181.

Bandler, R., & Grinder, J. (1975). *Patterns of the hypnotic techniques of Milton H. Erickson, M.D.* (Vol. 1). Cupertino, CA: Meta.

Barber, T. X., & Calverley, D. S. (1963). Toward a theory of hypnotic behaviour: Effects on suggestibility of task motivating instructions and attitudes towards hypnosis. *Journal of Abnormal and Social Psychology, 67*, 557–565.

Barber, T. X., & Calverley, D. S. (1964). Toward a theory of hypnotic behaviour: Effects on suggestibility of defining the situation as hypnosis and defining response to suggestion as easy. *Journal of Abnormal and Social Psychology, 68*, 585–592.

Barber, T. X., & De Moor, W. (1972). A theory of hypnotic induction procedures. *American Journal of Clinical Hypnosis, 15*(2), 112–135.

Barber, T. X., & Glass, L. B. (1962). Significant factors in hypnotic behaviour. *Journal of Abnormal and Social Psychology, 64*, 222–228.

Erickson, M. H. (1959). Further techniques of hypnosis: Utilization techniques. *American Journal of Clinical Hypnosis, 2*, 3–21.

Erickson, M. H. (1964). The confusion technique in hypnosis. *American Journal of Clinical Hypnosis, 6*, 183–207.

Erickson, M. H., & Rossi, E. L. (1979). *Hypnotherapy: An exploratory casebook*. New York: Irvington.

Erickson, M. H., & Rossi, E. L. (1980). Indirect forms of suggestion. In E. L. Rossi (Ed.), *The collected papers of Milton H. Erickson on hypnosis* (Vol. I, pp. 452–477). New York: Irvington.

Eysenck, H. J. (1947). *Dimensions of personality*. London: Routledge & Kegan Paul.

Hammer, A. G., Evans, F. J., & Bartlett, M. (1963). Factors in hypnosis and suggestion. *Journal of Abnormal and Social Psychology, 67*, 15–23.

Hilgard, E. R. (1967). Individual differences in hypnotizability. In J. E. Gordon (Ed.), *Handbook of clinical and experimental hypnosis* (pp. 391–443). New York: Macmillan.

Hilgard, E. R., & Hilgard, J. R. (1962). Developmental-interactive aspects of hypnosis: Some illustrative cases. *Genetic Psychology Monographs, 66*, 143–178.

Hilgard, J. R. (1970). *Personality and hypnosis: A study of imaginative involvement*. Chicago: University of Chicago Press.

Hull, C. L. (1933). *Hypnosis and suggestibility: An experimental approach*. New York: Appleton-Century-Crofts.

Melei, J., & Hilgard, E. R. (1964). Attitudes towards hypnosis, self-predictions, and hypnotic susceptibility. *International Journal of Clinical and Experimental Psychology, 12*, 99–108.

Moore, R. K. (1964). Susceptibility to hypnosis and susceptibility to social influence. *Journal of Abnormal and Social Psychology, 68*, 282–294.

Murphy, M. B. (1985). A linguistic structural model for the investigation of the effectiveness of indirect suggestion. Unpublished master's thesis, University of Auckland, New Zealand.

Sarbin, T. R., & Lim, D. T. (1963). Some evidence in support of the role-taking hypothesis in hypnosis. *International Journal of Clinical and Experimental Hypnosis, 11*, 98–103.

Weitzenhoffer, A. M., & Hilgard, E. R. (1959). *The Stanford hypnotic susceptibility scale, forms A and B.*. Palo Alto: Consulting Psychologists Press.

Weitzenhoffer, A. M., & Weitzenhoffer, G. B. (1958). Sex, transference, and susceptibility to hypnosis. *American Journal of Clinical Hypnosis, 1*, 15–24.

The Use of Hypnotic-Relaxation Cassettes in a Gynecologic-Obstetric Ward

Haim Omer, Ph.D., Adam Darnel, M.D.,
Nehama Silberman, M.A., Daphna Shuval, M.A.,
and Tzvi Palti, M.D.

Haim Omer received his Ph.D. from Hebrew University of Jerusalem where he is now an Instructor of Psychology. He has a number of publications on strategic therapy, hypnosis and medical psychology.

Omer and colleagues present an important study based upon the use of standard hypnotic procedures. Barber's Rapid Induction Analgesia was presented on tape cassettes for the alleviation of pain, anxiety and discomfort during labor and gynecological procedures. The results suggest that the tapes' effectiveness diminishes with the increase of both stress and the degree of clash between instruction and experience.

Clinicians favoring a personalized-individualized approach to hypnosis and hypnotherapy are often at odds with researchers favoring the use of a standard hypnotic protocol in the laboratory. Clinicians tend to emphasize that in the hypnotherapeutic interaction, therapists constantly match suggestions to clients' reactions. Standard hypnotic protocols, such as those delivered by tape-recorder, pose severe limitations on this continuous therapist/client interaction.

Milton H. Erickson, in particular, has voiced cogent criticisms of the standard-protocol approach. He has argued that many of the conclusions about hypnosis based on standard protocols can be discounted on the ground that many subjects were either not hypnotized or insufficiently hypnotized (Erickson, 1980). The reason for this is that since standard-protocol instructions could not pace or utilize the subjects' actual reactions, whenever there was a clash between hypnotic instructions and subjects' experiences, the result would be a reduction of hypnotic involve-

Address reprint requests to Haim Omer, Ph.D., Department of Psychology, Hebrew University of Jerusalem, Mt. Scopus, Jerusalem 91905, Israel.

ment. Another argument frequently voiced is that the therapist's presence is critical for therapeutic effectiveness since it poses a higher demand for clients' attention and without it clients will lack a feeling of personal reassurance.

Proponents of standard protocols, on the other hand, consider their approach amenable to scientific verification, whereas the personalized-individualized approach allows little scope for controlled investigation. From a practical point of view, the standard-protocol approach has a potential for automatization (and, therefore, for serving larger populations at lower costs), whereas the personalized-individualized approach demands the constant presence of an expert clinician with each client. Some evidence for the potentially wide applicability of standard protocols is provided by group and individual forms of hypnotic suggestibility tests, which are administered through a fixed and often automated hypnotic text (Shor & Orne, 1962; Weitzenhoffer & Hilgard, 1962). The fact that standard group administration is effective in producing many kinds of hypnotic phenomena suggests that standard hypnotherapy may also be possible.

In the following studies, a slightly modified automated version of Barber's Rapid Induction Analgesia (RIA) (Barber, 1977) was used in three conditions involving different levels of stress and of potential for clash between hypnotic instructions and subjects' experiences. The level of stress in a situation refers to that experienced at the time when the stressful procedure is taking place. The potential for clash between instructions and experiences is a function of the disparity between the instructions themselves and the mental and physical processes that the subject is concurrently experiencing. The potential for clash of situation is evident at the time the hypnotic instructions are being given. Thus, hypnotic suggestions of pleasure and relaxation given at home as a preparation for childbirth labor have a lower potential for clash than similar suggestions given during labor.

The standard-protocol and the personalized-individualized approaches give rise to different predictions for the therapeutic consequences of varying levels of stress and of potential for clash. Regarding levels of stress, the personalized-individualized approach predicts that the higher the situational stress, the more important the therapist's personal presence. In high-stress situations, the need for personal reassurance will increase and the potential usefulness of automated hypnosis will accordingly be reduced. The standard-protocol approach leads to no such prediction. The two approaches also give rise to different predictions concerning varying levels of potential for clash. In situations with a higher potential for clash, the personalized-individualized approach predicts a lowered effectiveness for automated treatments; not so the standard-protocol approach.

The following studies investigated the use of a tape-recorded hypnotic intervention in three different gynecologic-obstetric settings.

Overview

The first study used automated RIA with patients about to undergo salpingography (which is an intrusive roetgengrophy of the fallopian tubes). Patients were given cassettes while in the waiting room, in a manner similar to Barber's actual procedure (Barber, 1977). This was a situation of relatively moderate stress; although patients are usually quite anxious, the real amount of pain involved is small. This was also a situation of relatively low potential for clash between instructions and possible experiences, since the client is not undergoing the stressful procedure at the time she is hearing the instructions.

The second study used RIA as a preparation for labor. Women were given RIA cassettes for home practice. This was a situation of relatively high stress; in addition to considerable anxiety, the experience of labor is usually very painful. The potential for clash between instruction and patients' experiences was again relatively low, since at the time of the hypnotic exercises patients were not experiencing any highly stressful stimuli (practice was conducted at home, usually during the eighth month of pregnancy).

The third study used RIA cassettes with women during labor. This was a situation of both high stress and high potential for clash. The high potential for clash was created by the fact that the women attended to the analgesia instructions at a time when they were probably experiencing severe pain.

These studies were conducted from a position of belief in the usefulness of standard protocols. The desirability of automated hypnosis in a gynecologic-obstetric ward is very high since trained hypnotherapists are usually not available for personal administration. Furthermore, Barber's success with RIA, which is a quasi-standard procedure was highly encouraging. Previous research using automated hypnosis as an adjunct to personal hypnosis in cases of premature labor had shown that the cassettes were very well received (Omer et al., 1986). The research hypothesis was that the automated procedures would be considerably helpful in all three conditions.

Study 1

Thirty women about to undergo salpingography at the Hadassah Hospital, Mt. Scopus, Jerusalem, were given a RIA cassette to listen to while in the waiting room before the medical procedure. They were told that they would be given hypnotic-relaxation cassettes to listen to, that these cassettes would probably help in reducing their discomfort, and that they would be as much in control of the situation as they desired. Four women refused to listen to the cassette and were not included in any of the groups.

The experimental group was compared with 29 women undergoing the same procedure who were not given the cassette. Groups were comparable in terms of age and reason for the salpingography. In the control group there was a higher proportion of women who had previously been acquainted with the physician performing the examination (15, vs. 7 in the experimental group). Women in both groups were asked to fill in an analogue scale, in which they rated their level of pain, tension, fear or anxiety, and discomfort during the procedure. The rating scales were given immediately after the salpingography. The physicians had not been informed about which women had listened to the cassettes, nor were they involved in administering the posthypnotic cue. Experimental subjects were given the posthypnotic suggestion that upon entering the examination room and sitting down in the gynecological chair they would feel increasingly relaxed and comfortable. In addition to the subject self-ratings, the examining physicians were also asked to rate the women on the same analogue scale. A comparison between the two groups is shown in Table 1.

As can be seen, women in the experimental group reported significantly less pain, tension, and fear or anxiety than women in the control group. When physicians' evaluations were considered, however, no significant differences between the two groups were found, although the actual differences obtained were all in the same direction as in the self-evaluations. That is, they favored the experimental group. Because of this lack of significant differences in physicians' evaluations, we may consider the size of the therapeutic effect as no more than moderate.

Study 2

Forty-one women in their eighth month of pregnancy were contacted at their routine visit to the gynecologic-obstetric clinic and were given RIA cassettes (with slight modifications) to use as a preparation for labor. The function of the cassettes was explained in the same manner as in Study 1. About 20 women said they were not interested in participating and were not included in any of the groups. All women had already delivered one healthy baby before (the sample was thus limited so as to allow for statistical neutralization). They were compared to 48 controls of similar age and background who did not receive hypnotic cassettes. Women who

Table 1

Comparison of Means and Standard Deviations of Distress Reported in
Salpingography between a Group of Women Receiving RIA cassettes and
a Group of No-Treatment Controls.†

	RIA Group (n = 30)	Control Group (n = 29)	Student's t
Subjects' Evaluations			
Pain	$M = 38.4$ $SD = 25.0$	$M = 50.9$ $SD = 27.2$	1.83*
Tension	$M = 43.2$ $SD = 25.3$	$M = 57.5$ $SD = 27.0$	2.10*
Fear or anxiety	$M = 37.3$ $SD = 26.6$	$M = 53.0$ $SD = 26.5$	2.28*
Discomfort	$M = 41.0$ $SD = 26.5$	$M = 51.6$ $SD = 28.0$	1.49
Physicians' Evaluations			
Pain	$M = 36.7$ $SD = 29.8$	$M = 41.3$ $SD = 26.8$	0.63
Tension	$M = 43.7$ $SD = 27.1$	$M = 50.2$ $SD = 27.3$	0.93
Fear or anxiety	$M = 40.2$ $SD = 28.1$	$M = 44.8$ $SD = 28.6$	0.63
Discomfort	$M = 37.7$ $SD = 28.3$	$M = 37.7$ $SD = 26.4$	0.00

† The higher score on this analogue scale indicates greater discomfort in each of
the designated categories.

* $p<.05$, one-tailed.

gave birth via Cesarean section or who received an epidural in the current delivery or the delivery immediately prior were excluded from both groups.

In the day following the delivery, women were given a scale of 1 to 100 on which they were asked to rate themselves on the following variables: overall labor difficulty, pain during labor, pain at delivery, feeling of loss of control, tension, anxiety, and positive experience of delivery. Higher scores on this scale indicate greater discomfort in each of the designated categories. The women were asked to rate both their current delivery experience and their previous one. A comparison between groups is shown in Table 2.

As can be seen, automated hypnotherapy was ineffective for improving the subjective experience of women in the experimental group. This finding was contrary to research expectations. Its meaning will be considered in the discussion.

Table 2

Comparison of Mean Scores and Standard Deviations on Self-Reported Comfort of a Group of Women in Labor Receiving RIA (as a Preparation for Labor) with a Group of No-Treatment Controls

	RIA Group (n = 41)	Control Group (n = 48)	Student's t
Overall labor difficulty	$M = 44.7$ $SD = 27.0$	$M = 43.9$ $SD = 28.4$	0.13
Pain during labor	$M = 65.1$ $SD = 24.8$	$M = 66.5$ $SD = 27.8$	-0.25
Pain at delivery	$M = 81.3$ $SD = 19.9$	$M = 77.4$ $SD = 23.5$	0.83
Loss of control	$M = 29.3$ $SD = 27.6$	$M = 28.2$ $SD = 28.4$	0.18
Tension	$M = 45.6$ $SD = 30.5$	$M = 50.3$ $SD = 33.4$	-0.69
Anxiety	$M = 44.7$ $SD = 32.5$	$M = 46.2$ $SD = 31.5$	-0.21
Positive experience of delivery	$M = 20.3$ $SD = 27.9$	$M = 26.8$ $SD = 29.0$	-1.07

None of the differences reached significance.

An analysis of variance was performed with the last birth experience as a covariate in order to neutralize women's experiences of their previous deliveries. This was done because there might have been a self-selection into the experimental group of women tending to have more difficult deliveries. Such a bias would be detrimental to the experimental group. This analysis did not change any of the results. The difference between groups remained nonsignificant after neutralization of previous birth experience. The overall direction of results also remained unchanged.

Study 3

Forty-one women were given slightly modified versions of RIA cassettes to listen to during labor, immediately after admission to the delivery room of Hadassah Hospital, Mt. Scopus, Jerusalem. The use of the cassettes was explained in the same manner as in the previous studies. Twenty other women did not listen to the cassette and were not included in any of the groups. The reasons for their not listening were: 1) they had arrived at the delivery room too close to the actual birth so that there was no time to listen to the cassette; or 2) they had not wanted to listen. Approximately five additional women began listening but stopped midway, expressing unwillingness to continue. The 41 women were compared to 48 controls (the same as in Study 2). All women had given birth to at least one healthy baby before. As in Study 2, this requirement was in order to allow for a statistical neutralization of the women's individual tendency for more or less difficult deliveries. The day after delivery, all women were given the same scales of 1 to 100 as in Study 2. Women delivering via Cesarean section or who received an epidural in the current delivery or the immediately prior one were excluded. A comparison between groups is show in Table 3.

As can be seen, women in the experimental group fared significantly worse than women in the control group. An analysis of variance was performed with previous birth experience as a covariant. This was done to neutralize the women's individual tendency for more or less difficult deliveries. When the previous birth experience was neutralized there was no change in the significance of results. The experimental group still fared significantly worse in the same variables as before.*

---

* Both in Study 1 and Study 2 an analysis was carried out comparing only women who had undergone a preparation for childbirth course in the previous delivery; another analysis was performed comparing only those who had not undergone such a preparation course. Results remained unchanged. It should be noted that only about 20% of all women had ever had a preparation course.

Table 3

Comparison of Mean Scores and Standard Deviations on Self-Reported
Comfort of a Group of Women in Labor Receiving RIA (during Labor)
and a Group of No-Treatment Controls.

	RIA Group (n = 41)	Control Group (n = 48)	Student's t
Overall labor difficulty	$M = 60.6$ $SD = 24.1$	$M = 43.9$ $SD = 28.4$	2.96**
Pain during labor	$M = 64.4$ $SD = 20.1$	$M = 66.5$ $SD = 27.8$	0.40
Pain at delivery	$M = 83.9$ $SD = 16.7$	$M = 77.4$ $SD = 23.5$	1.55
Loss of control	$M = 43.4$ $SD = 32.1$	$M = 28.2$ $SD = 28.4$	2.38*
Tension	$M = 55.6$ $SD = 27.2$	$M = 50.3$ $SD = 33.4$	0.81
Anxiety	$M = 47.9$ $SD = 31.7$	$M = 46.1$ $SD = 31.4$	0.26
Positive experience of delivery	$M = 66.6$ $SD = 26.9$	$M = 79.5$ $SD = 21.4$	2.50

* $p<0.05$
** $p<0.005$

Discussion

The main findings can be summarized as follows: The automated RIA was found to be moderately effective for a low stress, low potential for clash situation such as salpingography. When actual stress became higher, as in preparation for childbirth, automated RIA was found to be ineffective. Finally, in a situation of high stress and high potential for clash, such as automated RIA during labor itself, the Ericksonian criticism manifested itself with a vengeance: standardized treatment was found to be clearly detrimental to patients.

One possible explanation for the findings of Study 3 is that the selection of subjects for the experimental group was biased, since women who delivered very close to hospitalization did not have time to listen to the cassette. In this manner, most of the very easy deliveries would be filtered out of the experimental group. However, about half of the women who were not included in the experimental group actually chose to be excluded and in a few cases said that the cassettes were disturbing for them. We may assume that if these women had remained in the experimental group, they might have heightened the discomfort ratings of the group. In this manner, some of the women who were not included had a negative effect on the experimental group, whereas others had a positive one. It is important to remember that neutralizing the women's individual tendencies for higher or lower distress levels (as was done in the analysis of variance) did not modify results in any way. For these reasons, explaining the findings in terms of sampling bias is probably unconvincing.

Due to the standardized intervention and self-rating, the results can not be attributed to experimenter effect or to demand characteristics. This can be seen since the results of the findings (from Studies 2 and 3) were contrary to the experimenters' expectations.

These data seem to indicate that an automated treatment will be less effective in situations of high stress (when personal reassurance is needed) and even less so in situations of high potential for clash. In the latter case, automated treatment may turn out to have a negative effect for patients. In situations of low stress and with a low potential for clash, automated hypnotherapy may be moderately effective. Unfortunately, these are not the conditions where effective hypnosis is most needed. Further research is needed in which a standard-hypnotic approach is compared to an Ericksonian approach in which utilization of client response can be implemented. This study did not compare automated treatment with individualized treatment; therefore, we cannot make any valid comparisons between the two approaches.

References

Barber, J. (1977). Rapid Induction Analgesia: A clinical report. *American Journal of Clinical Hypnosis, 19*, 138–147.

Erickson, M. H. (1980). *The collected papers of Milton H. Erickson, M.D., Vol II*. New York: Irvington.

Omer, H., Friedlander, D., & Palti, Z. (1986). Hypnotic-relaxation in the treatment of premature labor. *Psychosomatic Medicine, 48*, 351–361.

Shor, R. E., & Orne, E. C. (1962). *The Harvard Group Scale of Hypnotic Susceptibility, Form A*. Palo Alto, CA: Consulting Psychologists Press.

Weitzenhoffer, A., & Hilgard, E. P. (1962). *Stanford Hypnotic Susceptibility Scale, Form A and B*. Palo Alto, CA: Consulting Psychologists Press.

Hypnosis:
Innate Ability or Learned Skills?

Harriet E. Hollander, Ph.D., Lynn Holland, M.S.W., and John M. Atthowe, Jr., Ph.D.

Harriet E. Hollander, Ph.D. (University of Pittsburgh), is a Project Director at the University of Medicine and Dentistry of New Jersey-Community Mental Health Center at Piscataway, and is an adjunct in Psychiatry at the UMDNJ-Robert Wood Johnson Medical School. She has published on the topic of delinquency. Lynn Holland, M.S.W. (Rutgers University), is in private practice Metuchen, NJ, and John M. Atthowe, Jr., Ph.D. (Stanford University), is a Professor in the Department of Psychiatry, UMDNJ-Robert Wood Johnson Medical School.

Hollander, Holland and Atthowe discuss the issue of hypnotic ability versus skill. Subjects were tested on a standard scale for hypnotic suggestibility before and after a seminar on modern clinical hypnosis in therapy. Results indicate that while subjects did not improve from pre- to posttests on the standard scale, they did show increased hypnotic ability on similar items presented in the indirect Ericksonian format, which involved ideomotor tasks, imagery and dissociation. This pilot study raises interesting questions about indirect and direct suggestion.

The present investigation addresses the question "Who is hypnotizable?" by comparing subject responses to direct and indirect hypnotic approaches. It asks: Is hypnotic susceptibility a stable and reliable ability? Or is it a subtle, but ubiquitous, response tendency which is expressed in unique ways by each individual and depends upon the length of his or her experience and interaction with a creative operator?

The authors wish to acknowledge the constructive suggestions of Frederick J. Evans and Julie H. Wade, and to thank Lucille Carr-Kaffashan, Roberta Anderson, Lee S. Rosati, Sandra Long and Richard Thomas for their participation. The project was carried out with the support of the University of Medicine and Dentistry-Community Mental Health Center. Address reprint requests to Harriet E. Hollander, Ph.D., University of Medicine and Dentistry-Community Mental Health Center at Piscataway, Piscataway, NJ 08854.

In the last half of this century, two leading investigators of hypnotic phenomena, Ernest P. Hilgard and Milton H. Erickson, have been in intellectual opposition on the notion of hypnotizability. Although both men agree that hypnosis, when it occurs, is an altered state in which a secondary consciousness operates, Hilgard credits a hidden observer (Hilgard, 1977), whereas Erickson posits an unconscious in intense rapport with the hypnotist (Erickson, 1980a).

Hilgard (1981) has consistently described the hypnotic response as stable and reliable. He equates hypnotizability with the hypnotic talent of the subject and, with others, developed the Stanford Scales for its measurement (Weitzenhoffer & Hilgard, 1959, 1962, 1963). He considers the individual differences that emerge to be independent of the method of induction or an operator's personal characteristics (Hilgard, 1965, 1977, 1979, 1981, 1982). Erickson, on the other hand, states (1980c), "One hundred percent of normal people are hypnotizable," but adds, "It does not necessarily follow that one hundred percent are hypnotizable by any one individual." Ability depends on the situation and on the motivation of the patient. He stresses that subjects vary in their time requirements to achieve trance and to master different items, and questions the idea of an induction technique controlled as if it were a process apart from the subject's own behavior (Erickson, 1980d).

The research evidence supports both camps. Subjects do respond differentially to the Stanford Scales and find taking the Stanford a pleasant experience (Frankel, 1979). More than two-thirds of subjects experience "involuntariness" on passed item (Bowers, 1981). Stanford scores are stable over a 10-year period (Morgan et al., 1974). Perry (1977), summarizing the research on test-retest scores on the Stanford, concludes that without special interventions, susceptibility must be considered a stable characteristic of individuals. There is also evidence that special interventions can alter susceptibility scores. Several studies have shown that small but significant increments can be obtained in Stanford scores following therapeutic interventions, sensory isolation (Shor & Cobb, 1968), group process, drug use, or other mind altering procedures (Diamond, 1977). Burns (1977) found that with training, hypnotizability improved on specific groups of items such as ideomotor signalling, imagery, post-hypnotic hallucination and suggestion.

Whether hypnotizability is a fixed trait or something that can be learned has implication for decisions about clinical treatment. Hilgard and Hilgard (1975) carried out research on patient response to treatment for the alleviation of pain and found that Stanford scores predicted treatment outcome. Similar findings are reported for patients with anxiety and phobias (Frankel et al., 1979; Frischholz et al., 1971). These findings have not gone unquestioned. Barber (1980) has shown that low-hypnotizable pain patients, highly motivated to obtain relief, have been successfully treated under unlimited time conditions with indirect approaches. His research findings are supported by Alman (1980) and Matthews (1985).

The major challenge to the view that hypnotic ability is fixed and that its measurement predicts treatment was posed by the publication of Erickson's (1980) *Collected Papers*. The *Collected Papers*, together with Rossi's analysis of Erickson's methods (Erickson & Rossi, 1979, Erickson et al., 1976), the transcribed report of an Erickson training seminar (Zeig, 1980), and the evolution of further sophisticated techniques based on Erickson's teachings (Carter, 1983, Gilligan, 1986, Lankton & Lankton, 1983) require that attention be paid to hypnotizability as it occurs in the context of complex subject-operator interaction. Rossi (1986) has recently developed a scale to measure hypnotizability of subjects by indirect techniques in a clinical setting.

Disagreement over the relative contribution of innate endowment and skill training to hypnotic performance may reflect the differences obtained by operators in different contexts using different methods. Hilgard (1965, 1977, 1979, 1981, 1982) induces trance using a time-limited, standardized laboratory procedure and then observes how subjects respond to simply worded, direct, but unrelated challenges to respond hypnotically. Erickson (1980c) induced trance in a clinical, individually oriented manner. He gave ample time for trance development and found that if he utilized indirect, personally meaningful suggestions, his subjects could be trained to exhibit catalepsy, automatic writing, and arm levitation or could so vividly image these phenomena that they experienced them subjectively as really taking place.

Weitzenhoffer (1980), addressing the issues dividing laboratory oriented and clinically oriented hypnotists, asks: If hypnotizability is trainable, what skills are being trained? If it can be learned, is the idea of the coexistence of an innate skill ruled out? Can hypnotic behavior be understood separate from the context of the intense interpersonal experience in which it is conducted? Does responsiveness depend on whether subjects perceive themselves or others as being the controlling agents in trance experience?

The present study is an attempt to clarify the nature of hypnotic susceptibility through a comparison of traditional, direct procedures for evoking and measuring hypnotic susceptibility with indirect procedures which combine facilitation and utilization. Specifically, we were interested in exploring the differences and similarities in objective and subjective responses to direct and indirect hypnotic suggestions and in the transfer of response between the two conditions. We asked: Does becoming familiar with and practicing Ericksonian methods of hypnosis during 2½ days of formal and informal training change a person's hypnotic susceptibility as measured by a modified version of the Stanford Group Scales? To this end, we proposed a series of questions and framed a number of research hypotheses.

Hypothesis 1. There will be no difference between the administration of the modified Group Scale before and after a 2½-day workshop in the Ericksonian approach.

Is the Group Scale stable? Is susceptibility, as measured by the Group Scale, a more or less enduring trait?

Hypothesis 2. The test-retest reliability of the Group Scale, as measured by a Spearman rank order correlation, will not be significantly above chance and will not be able to account for at least 50% of the total variance.

Another major focus of the investigation was the comparison of the nature and type of hypnotic response to an Ericksonian training experience with a similar response to the Group Scales. Does the indirect approach tap a greater degree of susceptibility and a greater feeling of involvement than the direct measure?

Hypothesis 3. There will be no differences between the items passed or failed within an indirect, compared to a direct, induction procedure.

Hypothesis 4. There will be no differences among participants in their report of involvement with the indirect approach.

Can the validity of the concept of susceptibility be enhanced by asking each person to be more precise in describing their degree of response and to further describe their subjective experiences as they respond to each item, thereby increasing the richness of the response? As we seek greater richness, do we reduce the reliability of the response?

Hypothesis 5. There is no difference between a pass-fail and a four-point scoring system in terms of item variability and reliability.

Hypothesis 6. There is no difference between a person's subjective and objective response to a hypnotic suggestion.

The present research sought to compare subject responsiveness to direct and indirect induction approaches in an attempt to better understand "who is really hypnotizable."

Method

Subjects

Subjects were obtained from a 2½-day seminar taught by two of the authors, entitled "The Integration of Modern Hypnotic Technique into Clinical Practice." Twenty-eight of the seminar participants agreed to be research subjects. The seminar was offered to professional psychotherapists including psychiatrists, psychologists, clinical social workers, master's level nurses, and graduate students. Subjects were offered a reduced fee in exchange for participation in the study and keeping a journal of their experiences. The research method selected was designed to compare hypnotic performance on a modified version of the Stanford Scale of Hypnotizability with hypnotic performance during the course of the seminar in which Ericksonian techniques were introduced. The modified version of the Stanford Scale was prepared by one of the authors for group administration.

Procedures

Subjects were seated in two large semicircles, one behind the other. Each subject selected a seat and used the same seating position throughout the observed portions of the seminar. Subjects were assigned numbers for research identification and observation purposes. Trained observers were present throughout the seminar to record the presence or absence of desired hypnotic phenomena. Each observer was assigned to five or fewer subjects for the duration of the seminar. The observers had all been trained in hypnosis but were naive for the purpose of the investigation. They recorded on prepared checklists the hypnotic responses of their subjects during both administrations of the Stanford Group Scale and during the five group trance experiences presented during the training part of the program. Two video cameras were operated by technicians to cover the room and to provide a backup for verifying observation. Participants also recorded their subjective responses in a specially prepared booklet for the Stanford Scale and in a diary with questions for the training seminar.

To count a response to a hypnotic challenge as having occurred, agreement was needed between both a subject's journal report and rater observation. Videotapes were scanned to resolve disagreements. When the videotaped responses were also ambiguous, the hypnotic challenge was counted as failed.

A modified version of the Stanford Scale of Hypnotizability was given to the research subjects at the beginning and at the end of the seminar. The modified scale (Group Scale) included Hand Widening, Dream, Age Regression and other items derived from Stanford Scales A, B, C, and Clinical Scales (Hilgard, 1965, 1977, 1979, 1981, 1982; Hilgard & Hilgard, 1975). Subject response to both administrations of the Group Scale is summarized in Table 1. The Group Scale was administered by a clinician trained in the Stanford Scale hypnotic tradition.

The seminar itself was designed to introduce and train participants in trance induction and trance utilization using indirect methods. Topics were usually presented in didactic form followed by demonstrations of indirect technique and an opportunity for participants to practice the skills presented. Five group trance experiences were given by one or both of the instructors to facilitate integration of learning experiences. The training experiences were also used to indirectly elicit very similar or comparable phenomena obtained during the administration of the modified version of the Stanford Scale. All the phenomena sought during the training experience are described below. Table 2 compares hypnotic challenges given during training that are very similar to the Group Scale; Table 3 reports items that are comparable in the type of hypnotic response sought.

Hand Movement. Suggestions for hands moving apart were presented in a play format in which participants were given "permission" to explore their own capabilities and to allow themselves to have an enjoyable learning experience. Suggestions were woven into the text that perhaps subjects could experience the pulling of large magnets or the stretching of a rubber band or any other pulling force they might imagine.

Arm Rigidity. Suggestions for arm rigidity were presented during the above described exercise. Participants were encouraged to enjoy experiencing either arm as a rigid object, perhaps as a steel rod, baseball bat, hockey stick, or any other such object that the participant could imagine. It was further suggested that as long as one remained focused on the imagined object, the arm might be difficult or impossible to bend.

Fly on Nose (crawling insect). While subjects' arms were extended with an imagined heavy object in one hand and light object in the other, a story was told about what often happens when your hands are full and a fly or some other pesty insect or itch bothers your nose.

Visualizing Pleasant Place. In the course of discussing safety and autonomy, a suggestion was given indirectly to find a safe, pleasant place: "And you can trust yourself...to be a learner...from yourself...and trust depends on having a feeling of safety...and as you breathe...in and out...comfortably...knowing that you can take care of your sense of safety...with your breathing...letting yourself be safe enough to have an image...of interest...of thought...that you want to learn about. How do you know when you have an experience...an anchor of safety? Now, almost everyone has a place...or a sound...or a voice...or a relationship...or a place...they associate with pleasure and safety. For some people...it's a beach...a mountain...you can go wherever you want."

Age Regression (1). Suggestions were presented to the group integrating the use of stories and metaphors describing past memories and experiences as a means of eliciting regression to earlier years and to a variety of experiences.

Age Regression (2). Subjects were given a facial tissue to wad up in their hands together with the waking suggestions that holding something could revive experiences as with a transitional object. Part of the trance induction was as follows: "Can I?...It feels good to...let go a little...and remember a time when...sensory things were really important...movement...skills you acquire on a swing...climbing a tree...learning to swim...or you can stay on the shore or the edge of that pool and just see it from your safe place. You can separate and be apart from it... and let it come back to you safely...and there may be some elements of that experience...that, from your safe place here...you can let yourself know about...back there...in the classroom...the smell of chalk...the smell of something being baked in a kitchen...What color was your report card?...Who took you in to buy a pair of shoes?...Sneakers?"

Posthypnotic Suggestion for Dreams (night). Having a dream at night was indirectly suggested in the format of telling stories about dreams others have had, talking in general about dreams as a form of communication between the conscious and unconscious mind, and describing various ways in which people dream.

Hypnotic Dream (day). A hypnotic dream came after a suggestion for an age regression experience and was followed by a suggestion for posthypnotic amnesia for all or part of the trance. The cue for reversal of trance amnesia was given in an exercise scheduled on the following day.

Amnesia (specific). Specific amnesia was scored if, as suggested, subjects were unable to remember any details of the last group trance of the previous day (see above) or if the number of details reported in subjects' journals increased after the morning training exercise which included posthypnotic suggestions for removal of amnesia.

Amnesia (spontaneous). Credit was given for spontaneous amnesia if subjects clearly described an inability to remember most or all of any given group trance experience in the seminar.

Laughter (1). During a training session on how to "let go" in order to experience trance, suggestions were embedded in a story about how difficult it can be to stifle a giggle in a quiet place like a church, or to hold back a laugh, and what a relief it can be to finally let go and enjoy a belly laugh.

Laughter (2). Another laughter challenge consisted of telling a story about Norman Cousins and how he used comedy movie reruns to cheer himself up during recovery from a life-threatening illness. Themes of several funny movies, including a Marx Brothers film, were woven into the story.

Bird Visualization. Suggestions to visualize a bird in a garden were woven into the text of a story about how pain control was successfully accomplished for a terminally ill patient who concentrated on the beauty of her garden and its birds to distract her from pain.

Anosmia for Ammonia. Embedded in a trance in which subjects were told they would learn techniques for diminishing pain was the following trance suggestion: "You may want to show yourself, as you will show your patients in your office, that you can, while remaining deeply in trance, open up the cap on the ammonia bottle, sniff it, and just return it without experiencing that smell in any noxious way...just letting the bottle move slightly before your nose for a half second or so...just close to your chin and putting it down...that's fine, putting it down…and if you had the experience of not smelling the ammonia, it's really nice to know that you have that ability…and if you were able to perceive that smell now, just go back deeply into trance…knowing that any time as the trance continues, you can autonomously take the cover off the bottle and try it again and see if that learning will come to you later on…"

Automatic Writing. As part of an automatic writing experience, an eyes-open trance experience was offered as well as a chance to try automatic writing. Subjects were first invited to let their hand guide them in writing: "Some message…let your unconscious guide your hand."

Color Agnosia. The suggestion for agnosia was to "experience the forgetting of unimportant things" followed by suggestions interspersed throughout the trance "not to see" the color of the operator's dress. Subjects were then invited to try and write down the color of the operator's dress. The challenge was scored once for marked hesitation in writing down the color of the dress and a second time to note removal of agnosia. The standard for agnosia was failure to write the item on first request and success after being told that it was a nice surprise to remember forgotten things "like the color of L's dress."

Each reorientation was informal. Subjects were asked to reorient to their present surroundings in their own time and in their own way. In addition, a number of pauses were placed throughout the group trance to allow participants to develop their own unique inner experience.

The main outline of each group trance experience was prepared in advance but delivered extemporaneously. Certain item challenges were preselected for each trance to facilitate the task of the observers, but the operators remained sensitive to the mood of the group and the need to adjust the experience in terms of participants' expectation of learning to master and experiment with hypnotic phenomena. Trained observers recorded the presence or absence of desired phenomena during the administration of the Group Scale and the seminar experience, using a prepared rating form as an objective measure.

Subjective responses to the Group Scale for such items as the hypnotic dream, ammonia anosmia, age regression, visualizing pleasant place, and amnesia were recorded in a booklet especially designed for use with the modified Group Scale. Subjective responses to prepared questions for the group trance experiences and for specific item challenges embedded in them were recorded in a journal kept throughout the seminar.

Results

The intervention of a 2½-day Ericksonian training experience, in which participants were invited to explore their responses to hypnotic suggestion in their own way, did not significantly change the overall susceptibility of subjects to hypnosis, as measured by a pre- and postadministration of a modified version of the Stanford Group Scales (see Table 1). *Hypothesis 1* was accepted.

Table 1

Comparison of First and Second Administration of Group Scale

| | Percent Passing | |
Items	1st Adm.	2nd Adm.
Hands apart or together	43	89
Dream	39	46
Age regression (2nd & 5th grade)	25	21
Tactile & auditory hallucinations (mosquito)	39	36
Visual hallucination (mosquito)	11	18
Anosmia for ammonia	7	7
Agnosia to pencil	14	0
Viewing funny scene (imagery)	29	14
Relaxing at beach (imagery)	46	46
Posthypnotic suggestion (cough)	7	7
Amnesia	0	4

Rs = 0.732 Mean 1 = 2.5 Mean 2 = 2.9

One of the 11 items did show significant change. On the posttest, the hand movement challenge was passed by 89% of the participants, as compared with 43% who passed the item on the pretest ($p<.005$). The test of significance used throughout this paper is the McNemar Test for the Significance of Changes, which approximates the chi square distribution with one degree of freedom. All tests of significance were two-tailed.

Hypothesis 2 was rejected. Hypnotic susceptibility, as measured in the present study by the Group Scale, was reliable. The test-retest reliability of the modified Group Scales, measured 2 days apart, was 0.732, accounting for 54% of the variance in common, which is significantly above chance

($p<.001$). Reliability was assessed by the Spearman Rank Correlation Coefficient corrected for ties.

Hypothesis 3 was rejected. In the indirect approach used in the training seminar, most participants passed more than half of challenges similar to those on the Group Scale. Those participants who changed their scores passed significantly more items than they failed ($p<.001$).

Our participants would be considered low hypnotizables (Atthowe & Roder, 1986). Only one participant passed more than half of the Group Scale items. Yet, in 17 of 19 indirect challenges, the participants showed increased hypnotizability as compared to their first Group Scale score ($p<.001$). All nine indirect challenge items, which were comparable to direct Group Scales challenges, were changed in a positive direction by the participants ($p<.01$). As Table 2 shows, subjects were much more likely to react to age regression, posthypnotic suggestion, amnesia, and response to a funny scene (laughter 2) in indirect than direct inductions. Hands moving apart or together, tactile and visual hallucinations showed no differences. All items showed positive changes (i.e., more people passing the item). Table 3 indicates that an additional tactile hallucination (experiencing a crawling insect) was not significantly changed by the indirect chal-

Table 2

Changes in Number of Participants Passing or Not Passing Items during Indirect Inductions, as Compared to Their Group Scale I Scores*

Items	Change Scores		
	Passed	Not Passed	Level of Significance
Hands apart	10	4	n.s.
Age regression (1)	12	1	0.01
Age regression (2)	21	1	0.001
Tactile hallucination (fly)	6	3	n.s.
Visual hallucination (bird)	9	2	0.08
Smile (funny movie, TV)	10	0	0.01
Posthypnotic suggestion	25	0	0.001
Amnesia (posthypnotic)	17	0	0.001
Anosmia (ammonia)	7	5	n.s.
Total Changes	117	16	0.001

*Item challenges were very similar in both situations.

Table 3

Changes in Number of Participants Passing or Not Passing Items during
Indirect Inductions, as Compared to Their Group Scale I Scores*

| | Change Scores | | |
Items	Passed	Not Passed	Level of Significance
Arm rigidity	12	0	0.005
Dream (day)	4	7	n.s
Dream (posthypnotic)	5	4	n.s.
Amnesia (spontaneous)	22	0	0.001
Tactile hallucination (crawling insect)	3	8	n.s.
Agnosia (color)	8	2	n.s.
Agnosia (hesitation in automatic writing)	16	3	0.01
Relaxation scene (safe place)	13	2	0.01
Smile (stifle giggle)	9	3	n.s.
Total Changes	100	32	0.001

* Item challenges were comparable in both situations.

lenge. Subjects were more likely to fail the tactile item with an indirect approach. Suggestions to dream also did not show a change, possibly due to our inadvertent error in suggesting a dream in a trance along with repeated suggestions for trance amnesia. Spontaneous amnesia, which seems to be associated with a somnambulistic state, was reported by 79% of the participants during the training seminar. No subject demonstrated amnesia on the Group Scale ($p<.001$). Agnosia for the color blue was found more frequently in the indirect approach and showed a significant change, manifested by marked disruption or hesitation in writing, as rated by observers ($p<.01$).

Hypothesis 4 was rejected. Of the 28 participants, five (18%) felt greater satisfaction and involvement with the Group Scale (e.g., they were better able to relax). The overwhelming majority (79%) preferred the indirect or Ericksonian approach ($p<.001$), and one participant indicated that the two approaches were about the same. The main reasons for preferring the indirect approach were: it is more comfortable (25%); it is less authoritarian (14%); and participants felt less resistance (14%). Most participants felt the indirect approach was more fun. Some people said they felt more anxious when responding to direct suggestions.

Hypothesis 5 was accepted. When we compared the new four-point scoring system with the traditional pass-fail, there was only a slight difference in reliability between the two methods of scoring. The pass-fail test-retest reliability was 0.67, compared to 0.74 for the four-point system. This difference did not approach significance. Both methods of scoring produced stable results. However, there was almost twice as much variability when the four-point system was used, attesting to greater richness.

Hypothesis 6 was also accepted. In comparing the participants' subjective reports of their performance with the objective observations of an observer (backed by the video camera), we found no significant differences. Only 11% of the responses differed. Most of these changes were with the hand movement item (36%). Participants reported a greater response to motor and dissociative items than was reflected in observer ratings. Some participants felt they did more poorly, mostly in the hallucinatory suggestions. Differences in subjective and objective reports were also found by Sheehan and McConkey (1982), but none of the differences in the present study reached significance.

Discussion

The results of this study show that hypnotic ability, under certain conditions, appears to be a stable characteristic of individuals and that, under other conditions, hypnotic performance can be significantly augmented.

On the one hand, the prevailing view that hypnotic scores are stable was upheld in this study. There was no significant change in participants' response to the modified version of the Stanford Group Scale following a 2½-day training experience with Ericksonian approaches to hypnosis. On the other hand, the results show that when permissive, personally oriented trance inductions are employed, subjects respond to a fairly wide range of hypnotic suggestion.

Although only a few subjects responded to hypnotic challenges for tactile hallucination, agnosia, or negative hallucination (anosmia for ammonia), subjects showed a positive and significant level of response to items involving imagery and dissociation, and appeared to be in fairly deep states of trance.

Were these subjects responding to the implicit contextual suggestion that Ericksonian approaches were somehow more desirable than direct approaches? Were they a self-selected group whose attendance at the seminar implied they were predisposed to Ericksonian methods? We did not have a control group specifically encouraged to find a basis for preferring direct induction procedures. Still, it seems unlikely that our subject's performance was a response only to the demand characteristic of the situation or to the different characteristics of the operators.

Those who attended the workshop were naïve about its specific investigative purpose. In fact, our participants, who were sophisticated mental health professionals, might have been expected to show a performance increment during the second administration of the Group Scale. Such a performance increment would have reflected their positive skill training and a desire to please the trainers of the workshop. However, there was no reliable change between the first and second administration of the Group Scale.

Were they asleep during the Erickson training? The evidence suggests they were not. They responded to interspersed suggestions to produce trance phenomena and showed the typical features associated with trance. In fact, 20 of the 28 subjects exhibited the classic features of somnambulism. Somnambulism was originally defined by Liebault (Bernheim, 1880) as a deep stage of hypnosis. This trance state is characterized by forgetfulness upon waking of all that has happened. Bernheim (1880), extending Liebault's observations, notes that suggestibility is most marked among somnambulists who are amnesic for trance. He further observes that the suggestibility phenomenon is not constant and that amnesia upon waking may be the only symptom characteristic of somnambulism.

Our subjects, though often unresponsive to suggestions for catalepsy or automatic movements, did show posthypnotic responsivity and partial or full spontaneous amnesia. They reported in their diaries and commented in the videotaped group discussions that they were in a "sleep state," "out of it," "in trance," "aware of a voice but not the content," and that they were often oblivious to suggestions presented during the trance.

For Hilgard (1977), somnambulism is synonymous with hypnotic virtuosity, but only when accompanied by high suggestibility for catalepsy, ideomotor activity, and hallucinosis. This restrictive definition may fail to include some highly hypnotizable subjects. There was a vivid example of such undermeasurement in the workshop. During training one subject failed the challenge to visualize a bird. She wrote in the recall section of her diary, "What bird?" Yet during trance, she had responded to the automatic writing challenge by drawing on the previous page a simple, but unmistakable representation of a bird. Her Stanford scores on both administrations were low.

Since subjects were both hypnotizable and suggestible during the workshop, why was this performance superiority not transferred to the Group Scale on retest? Possible explanations are that a period of consolidation was needed before retest, or that as there was a genuine preference for an indirect, permissive, personally oriented trance experience over a direct, authoritarian demand that subjects respond to disconnected challenges. The present findings are consistent with Weitzenhoffer's (1980) observation that hypnotic conditions differ depending on whether or not subjects perceive themselves as controlling agents.

If trance is inseparable from its interpersonal context, as Erickson and Weitzenhoffer have argued, the question as to whether hypnotizability is a stable characteristic within subjects may not be answerable. The Heisenberg paradox (Capra, 1976) recognizes that procedures change the nature of the object that is being measured. The rules of modern scientific logic do not require an untangling of the lines separating subject and operator to the extent they form a single context. From such a perspective, it is reasonable to explore the limits of individual hypnotizability under a variety of conditions, giving consideration to the identification of optimal circumstance, operator skill, and variation of time needed to achieve altered states.

The present findings support this kind of investigative approach. They indicate that the context in which suggestions are put forth does influence the nature of hypnotizability. In this study we have observed that low hypnotizable participants perform surprisingly better in demonstrating hypnotic phenomena when operators believe that they are emphasizing autonomy, are giving permission to explore an altered state, and are encouraging subjects to experience a meaningful connection with deeper levels of personal awareness. The evidence has implications for making judgments about treatment amenability based on traditional evaluations using a direct approach.

References

Alman, B. M., & Carney, R. E. (1980). Consequences of direct and indirect suggestions on success of posthypnotic behavior. *American Journal of Clinical Hypnosis*, 22(2), 112–118.

Atthowe, J. & Roder, G. (1986). Personal communication.

Barber, J. (1980). Hypnosis and the unhypnotizable. *The American Journal of Clinical Hypnosis*, 23(1), 4–9.

Bernheim, H. (1880). *Suggestive therapeutics: A treatise on the nature and uses of hypnotism*. New York and London: G. P. Putman's Sons.

Bowers, K. S. (1981). Do the Stanford Scales tap the "classic suggestion?" *The International Journal of Clinical and Experimental Hypnosis*, 29(1), 47–53.

Burns, A. (1977). The distribution and factor structure of hypnosis scores following intervention. *The International Journal of Clinical and Experimental Hypnosis*, 35(3), 192–201.

Capra, F. (1976). *The tao of physics*. New York: Bantam Books.

Carter, P. (1983). The parts model. Unpublished doctoral dissertation. Los Angeles: International College.

Erickson, M. E. (1980a). A brief survey of hypnotism. In E. Rossi (Ed.), *Hypnotic investigation of psychodynamic processes*. New York: Irvington.

Erickson, M. E. (1980b). Deep hypnosis and its induction. In E. Rossi (Ed.) *The nature of hypnosis and suggestion*. New York: Irvington.

Erickson, M. H. (1980c). *The collected papers of Milton H. Erickson*. (Vols. I–IV, E. Rossi, Ed.). New York: Irvington.

Erickson, M. H. & Rossi, E. L. (1979). *Hypnotherapy*. New York: Irvington.

Erickson, M. H., Rossi, E. L., & Rossi, S. I. (1976). *Hypnotic realities*. The induction of clinical hypnosis and the indirect forms of suggestion. New York: Irvington.

Frankel, F. H. (1979). Scales measuring hypnotic responsivity: A clinical perspective. *The American Journal of Clinical Hypnosis, 21*(2 & 3), 208–217.

Frankel, F. H., Apfel, R. J., Kelly, S. F., Benson, H., Quinn, T., Newmark, J., & Malmaud, R. (1979). The use of hypnotizability scales in the clinic: A review after six years. *The International Journal of Clinical and Experimental Hypnosis, 27*(2), 63–73.

Frischholz, E. J., Spiegel, H., & Spiegel, D. (1981). Hypnosis and the unhypnotizable: A reply to Barber. *American Journal of Clinical Hypnosis, 24*(1), 55–59.

Gilligan, S. G. (1986). *Therapeutic trances: The cooperation principle in Ericksonian hypnotherapy*. New York: Brunner/Mazel.

Hilgard, E. R. (1965). *Hypnotic susceptibility*. New York: Harcourt Brace & World.

Hilgard, E. R. (1977). *Divided consciousness*. New York: John Wiley.

Hilgard, E. R. (1979). The Stanford Hypnotic Susceptibility Scales as related to other measures of hypnotic responsiveness. *The American Journal of Clinical Hypnosis, 21*(2 & 3), 68–82.

Hilgard, E. R. (1981). Hypnotic susceptibility under attack: An examination of Weitzenhoffer's criticisms. *The International Journal of Clinical and Experimental Hypnosis, 29*(1), 21–41.

Hilgard, E. R. (1982). Susceptibility and implications for measurement. *International Journal of Clinical and Experimental Hypnosis, 30*(4), 394–403.

Hilgard, E. R., & Hilgard, J. R. (1975). *Hypnosis in the relief of pain*. Los Altos, CA: William Kaufman.

Lankton, C. & Lankton, S. (1983). *The answer within: A clinical framework of Ericksonian hypnotherapy*. New York: Brunner/Mazel.

Matthews, W. J. (1985). Indirect vs. direct hypnotic suggestions—an initial investigation. A brief communication. *The International Journal of Clinical and Experimental Hypnosis, 33*(3), 219–223.

Morgan, A. H., Johnson, D. L., & Hilgard, E. R. (1974). The stability of hypnotic susceptibility: A longitudinal study. *International Journal of Clinical and Experimental Hypnosis, 22*, 249–257.

Perry, C. W. (1977). Is hypnotizability modifiable? *The International Journal of Clinical and Experimental Hypnosis, 25*(3), 125–146.

Rossi, E. L. (1986). The Indirect Trance Assessment Scale (ITAS). In M. Yapko (Ed.), *Hypnotic and strategic interventions: Principles and practice*. New York: Irvington.

Sheehan, P. W., & McConkey, K. M. (1982). *Hypnosis and experience: The exploration of phenomena and process*. Hillsdale: Lawrence Erlbaum.

Shor, R. E., & Cobb, J. C. (1968). An exploratory study of hypnotic training using the concept of plateau responsiveness as a referent. *The American Journal of Clinical Hypnosis, 10*(3), 178–193.

Weitzenhoffer, A. M. (1980). Hypnotic susceptibility revisited. *The American Journal of Clinical Hypnosis, 22*(3), 130–146.

Weitzenhoffer, A. M., & Hilgard, E. R. (1959). *Stanford Hypnotic Susceptibility Scale, Forms A and B.* Palo Alto: Consulting Psychologists Press.

Weitzenhoffer, A. M., & Hilgard, E. R. (1962). *Stanford Hypnotic Susceptibility Scale, Form C.* Palo Alto: Consulting Psychologists Press.

Weitzenhoffer, A. M., & Hilgard, E. R. (1963). *Stanford profile scales of hypnotic susceptibility, Forms I and II.* Palo Alto: Consulting Psychologists Press.

Zeig, J. (1980). *A teaching seminar with Milton Erickson.* New York: Brunner/Mazel.

Comparisons

The Utilization of Cognition in Psychotherapy: A Comparison of Ericksonian and Cognitive Therapies

Jeffrey B. Feldman, Ph.D.

Jeffrey B. Feldman, Ph.D. (Case Western Reserve University) is in private practice in New York City. In addition to serving as a consulting psychologist to agencies located in New York City, he is a member of the faculty and Administrative Vice President of the New York Milton H. Erickson Society for Psychotherapy and Hypnosis. Previous publications include "Subliminal Perception and Information Processing Theory: Empirical and Conceptual Validation of Erickson's Notion of the Unconscious," which was corecipient of the Foundation's award for most scholarly accepted paper at the 1983 Erickson Congress.

Feldman compares and contrasts Ericksonian therapy with the cognitive model of Aaron Beck. Proposed is an information processing model which can serve as a bridge between the two approaches. In clinical practice, techniques from both schools can be used to enhance therapeutic effectiveness.

There is nothing good or bad but that thinking makes it so.
Shakespeare, Hamlet I.V. 259

The mind's its own place and in itself can make a Heaven of Hell a Hell of Heaven.
Milton, Paradise Lost 1.24'9

In preparing to write this chapter, I recalled a repeated early trance-like experience. When I was a child my mother often played for me a record, "The Little Engine that Could." Sung by Burl Ives, it told the story of a train that had to scale a steep hill before the toys on it could be delivered to the children awaiting them. Large engines could not climb the hill with such a heavy load and laughed at the little engine that wanted to try. The

---

Address reprint requests to Jeffrey B. Feldman, Ph.D., 1230 Park Avenue, #16A, New York, NY 10128.

little engine repeated the phrase, "I think I can, I think I can" as it worked its way up and over the hill. The moral of the story was explicit: "You can do most anything if you only think you can." With attention absorbed by Burl Ives' resonant voice, and visualizing the little engine chugging up the hill, I was in a form of trance. In addition to the obvious power of positive-thinking message, implicit in the song is the premise that our thoughts and underlying beliefs have a powerful effect on our behavior and affect.

It now appears that the psychotherapy field is catching up with Shakespeare, Milton, and the "Little Engine That Could." Two of the most important trends in psychotherapy are the Ericksonian movement, which emphasizes the use of trance, and the cognitive movement, which empha-sizes changing automatic thoughts and underlying belief structures. These movements developed independently from vastly different theoretical origins. Nevertheless, as an Ericksonian psychotherapist I have increas-ingly found myself using and combining techniques from both orienta-tions. This chapter, which began as an attempt to integrate methodologies, evolved into an effort at clinical and theoretical rapprochement between these two therapeutic trends.

Assuming a knowledge of Ericksonian therapy, this chapter first pres-ents a brief summary of cognitive therapy. Then, the wide range of simi-larities in practice and techniques used in cognitive and Ericksonian ther-apy are discussed. Differences in therapeutic principles are evaluated. Next, an information-processing model is presented as a theoretical bridge between these two approaches. Finally, the strengths of each approach, mutually enriching each other in this broader perspective, are discussed as part of a more complete therapeutic orientation.

Cognitive Therapy

Cognitive therapy, or cognitive-behavioral therapy, is a rubric designat-ing many therapeutic approaches with the underlying assumption that affect and behavior are largely determined by the way in which an indi-vidual construes the world (Turk et al., 1983, p. 4). The foremost practition-ers of this approach are Aaron Beck, who is most associated with the term "cognitive therapy," Donald Meichenbaum, often associated with the term "cognitive-behavioral therapy," and Albert Ellis who has developed "ra-tional-emotive therapy." Aside from Ellis, cognitive therapy has its roots largely in behavioral psychology, having created a revolution in that movement. One of the major emphases of behavioral psychology carried over to cognitive therapy is an empirical approach which has generated a great deal of research in support of its tenets. As will be seen, this empirical orientation is even taught to patients. This chapter focuses most upon

Beck's work (cf. Beck et al., 1979) because it has the greatest amount of supporting research; it seems to have the most broad-based appeal among cognitive therapists; and it may be the most generative of therapeutic strategies and techniques.

To begin the process of cognitive restructuring, Beck's depressed patients are given homework. They are to behave in such a way that new consequences will be incompatible with prior expectations. Taught that thoughts are hypotheses, patients are encouraged to evaluate those thoughts based on the data generated by the homework experience. In light of the new experience, therapeutic work augments changing these thoughts in terms of their associated expectations, appraisals, attributions, and images. Then patients learn to identify and change the underlying assumptions (Ellis' irrational beliefs, Beck's cognitive schemas) which generated the old self-defeating cognitions. Finally, patients are taught coping skills to help them apply these new beliefs in the environment (Beck et al., 1979). The process of encouraging patients to test their beliefs and apply their new cognitions in practical behaviors in the environment is one reason this therapeutic approach is often termed "cognitive-behavioral."

Both the cognitive and behavioral dimensions are also apparent in the therapeutic process developed by Beck and his associates for treating anxiety disorders. Patients are first taught to recognize the automatic thoughts that accompany their anxiety. Once able to recognize these thoughts, they are instructed to keep track of them in a notebook (i.e., collect data). They are next encouraged to carry out strategies for testing the veracity of these thoughts and beliefs about what might happen to them. In other words, a young man afraid to ask a woman for a date would be directed to ask her—not to actually get the date but to test his ability to ask. His exaggerated ideas about the probability of being rejected and his beliefs about how rejection will affect him are also examined by this exercise. Patients are taught to evaluate their thinking and identify their underlying assumptions based on data from homework experiments. A part of this ongoing evaluative process is the teaching of behavioral techniques for coping with the affective, behavioral and cognitive aspects of their anxiety as clients increasingly involve themselves in formerly anxiety-provoking situations (Beck & Emery, 1985, pp. 318–319).

Similarities in Therapeutic Approach

The conduct of therapy as practiced by a cognitive therapist initially may seem vastly different from the Ericksonian approach. Yet an examination of various aspects of the therapeutic approaches reveals a surprising number of similarities.

The stance of the therapist is one area of similarity, which might surprise some. While the cognitive approach may sound mechanistic, Beck, in a manner which captures the essence of an Ericksonian utilization approach, speaks of the importance of entering the patient's perspective and utilizing the patient's world view and idiosyncratic concepts (Beck et al., 1979, p. 143). Also, it is suggested that a patient's adaptive beliefs be utilized in changing dysfunctional beliefs and that "even the most difficult patient has strengths that can be used to offset antitherapeutic reactions" (Beck et al., 1979, p. 296). Similarly, cognitive therapists are instructed to gear their approach to the level of the patient (Beck et al., 1979, p. 169; Turk et al., 1983, p. 281) and to individually tailor therapeutic interventions for their patients (Turk et al., 1983, p. 347). Furthermore, while a specific sequential therapeutic process often is emphasized in cognitive therapy, flexibility, a hallmark of the Ericksonian approach (Lankton & Lankton, 1983, p. 21), is also described as being of great importance (Beck et al., 1979, p. 306). In addition, cognitive therapists are instructed to use "selective self-disclosure" in the form of telling stories about themselves (utilizing oneself) to activate affect in a patient (Beck et al., 1979, p. 171). Thus, certain hallmarks of the Ericksonian approach are also encouraged in the approach of the cognitive therapist, including meeting the patient at his or her model of the world, utilizing a patient's beliefs and strengths, individually tailoring therapy to the patient, utilizing oneself as a therapist, and flexibility.

Areas of similarity can also be found in therapeutic tactics. In a manner similar to Ericksonian strategic therapy, cognitive therapy begins by selecting symptoms that appear most amenable to change (Beck et al., 1979, p. 168). Similarly, in generating minimal strategic change, which is characteristic of Ericksonian therapy (Feldman, 1985a, p. 155), in cognitive therapy a large task is divided into small steps and a relatively easy first step is given to the patient for a start (Beck et al., 1979, p. 133). This is what the Lanktons (1983, p. 23) refer to as reducing a task to component bits.

While indirect suggestion is often associated with Ericksonian therapy, the Ericksonian therapist actively takes responsibility for therapeutic change, often directing the patient to take some specific action (Feldman, 1985a, p. 155). Erickson believed that patients learn best when they do things (Zeig, 1986, p. 254). There is no doubt that cognitive therapy is active and directive (Beck et al., 1979, p. 246), and one characteristic strongly associated with Milton Erickson—persistence—is actively encouraged by cognitive therapists (p. 296).

Another major area of overlap between cognitive and Ericksonian therapy is that of therapeutic techniques: Reframing is a technique used in cognitive therapy. For instance, if a patient "fails" at a task, it is reframed positively as a source of data for devising other projects (Beck et al., 1979, p. 134). Indeed, one can argue that cognitive therapy is a structured format for reframing an individual's cognitions. Metaphor is another technique used in cognitive therapy; therapists are instructed to use an "analogy which fits the patient" (Beck et al., 1979, p. 275, Turk et al., 1983, pp. 187–188). Beck and Emery (1985, p. 185) further instruct therapists that "when the patient is highly defended against learning new material, an indirect approach may have to be used by providing information, and using stories and metaphors (see also Rosen, 1982). Without calling it such, trance is used by cognitive therapists in their relaxation and imagery techniques. Such cognitive behavior techniques as cognitive rehearsal (Beck et al., 1979, p. 136) and imagery rehearsal (Turk et al., 1983, pp. 3–5) are termed "future pacing" by some Ericksonians. Similarly, induced imagery, time projection and symbolic imagery (metaphors) are familiar techniques to the Ericksonian practitioner of trance (see Beck & Emery, 1985, pp. 211, 216, 218). Furthermore, Emery specifically cites Erickson as a model for the therapeutic technique of "doing the unexpected" (Beck & Emery, 1985, p. 286)!

The rationale for Ericksonian behavioral interventions and the conceptualization of the resulting therapeutic process, as delineated by Gordon and Myers-Anderson (1981), is remarkably similar to those given by cognitive therapists. They delineate premises for Erickson's behavioral interventions as follows:

1) Because people's behaviors are patterned, any change in that pattern will result in new interactions and experiences;
2) Patterns of behavior are perpetuated by the corresponding chains of environmental feedback created by those new behaviors;
3) It is unnecessary to delve into the ontogeny of a problem in order to effect a profound and lasting change;
4) There is a correspondence between one's model of the world and behavior such that altering one's behavior has a direct impact on the individual's experience and generalizations. (cited by O'Hanlon, 1985, p. 47)

One can see that the cognitive model of change, with its emphasis upon initial behavioral intervention, is highly compatible with this model of Ericksonian behavioral intervention.

Differences and Similarities in Therapeutic Principles

In order to elucidate the differences between Ericksonian and cognitive therapies and, in the process, to further familiarize the reader with cognitive therapy, fundamental principles of cognitive therapy will be examined. These principles, as delineated by Emery, are:

1. Cognitive therapy is based on the cognitive model of emotional disorders.
2. Cognitive therapy is brief and time-limited.
3. A sound therapeutic relationship is a necessary condition for effective cognitive therapy.
4. Therapy is a collaborative effort between therapist and patient.
5. Cognitive therapy uses primarily the Socratic method.
6. Cognitive therapy is structured and directive.
7. Cognitive therapy is problem-oriented.
8. Cognitive therapy is based on an educational model.
9. The theory and techniques of cognitive therapy rely on the inductive method.
10. Homework is a central feature of cognitive therapy. (Beck & Emery, 1985, p. 167)

In comparing these principles with those of Ericksonian therapy, they will be classified as being either compatible with Ericksonian therapy, providing little fundamental conflict in viewpoint, or as diametrically opposed.

Compatible principles include principles 3 and 4 because virtually all schools of therapy agree upon the importance of a sound therapeutic relationship and that therapy is a collaborative effort between therapist and patient. Principle 10 is also compatible with Ericksonian therapy in that homework or therapeutic tasks are, as indicated above, an essential feature of Ericksonian strategic therapy. The fact that Ericksonian therapy is also problem-oriented makes it compatible with principle 7.

Concerning principle 2, while not all Ericksonian therapists would describe their approach as brief and time-limited, some would, especially the strategic therapists. In any case, Ericksonian therapy strives to help the patient resolve his or her presenting problem as quickly as possible and get on with life. The door is left open for future work if needed. In that sense, it is brief.

Concerning principle 6, while one of Erickson's major contributions to hypnosis and psychotherapy is the use of indirect suggestion, Erickson could also be highly directive (Grodner, 1986, p. 249). While neither the conduct of individual sessions nor the sequence of his therapeutic sessions were structured in the manner of cognitive therapy, Erickson often carefully planned his therapeutic interventions.

In elucidating principle 8, Beck and Emery explain, "A premise of cognitive therapy is that one develops anxiety not because of unconscious motivations but because one has learned inappropriate ways of handling life experience. This premise suggests that with practice one can learn more effective ways of leading one's life" (1985, p. 186). Similarly in describing principles of Ericksonian therapy, the Lanktons indicate that "given a person's particular frame of reference and history of learning, even a 'problem' behavior or feeling is the best choice a person has learned to make in a particular circumstance." They argue that if a person is confident in one situation but not another it "is not because s/he is resistant or has an investment in not succeeding. Rather, in Erickson's belief system, it is because the person has not learned the associational mechanisms to pull that confidence into the foreground when it is desired" (Lankton & Lankton, 1983, p. 13). Thus, while the emphasis in cognitive therapy is upon learning coping skills and new ways of thinking, and in Ericksonian therapy upon accessing and utilizing resources, they both involve corrective learning experiences. Furthermore, while somewhat different in emphasis, both therapeutic processes involve what Emery calls "learning to learn" (Beck & Emery, 1985, p. 186). Finally, the kind of didactic techniques advocated by Emery, such as providing information, assigning reading, listening to audiotapes, or suggesting that a patient attend a lecture, are similar to those prescribed at times by Erickson. In sum, while cognitive therapists tend to be more didactic in style, an educational model is not fundamentally at odds with an Ericksonian viewpoint.

We come then to those principles of cognitive therapy which seem diametric to Ericksonian therapy. In describing the first principle of cognitive therapy, Emery indicates that not only is the cognitive model used as a basis for intervention, but it is explicitly given to the patient as the rationale for treatment. In the first session, and thereafter, the therapist instructs the patient in the cognitive tenet that anxiety is maintained by a mistaken or dysfunctional appraisal of a situation (Beck & Emery, 1985, p. 168).

In a previous paper, I describe Ericksonian therapy as having an anthropological rather than a missionary approach. Instead of converting the patient to a system of beliefs and teaching him a format with which to describe himself and the world, it is the job of the therapist to learn the language of the patient, to adapt to and utilize the patient's reality (Feldman, 1985a, p. 154). In Erickson's words: "Each person is a unique individual. Hence psychotherapy should be formulated to meet the individual's needs rather than tailoring the person to fit the procrustean bed of a hypothetical theory of human behavior" (quoted in Zeig, 1982, p. 8). While cognitive therapy might use the patient's language and reality, its first goal is to instruct and commit the patient to the cognitive model of change. It is essential to develop within the patient a mental set which can enable him or her to notice and correct faulty thinking which leads to anxiety or depression.

The importance to cognitive therapy of establishing with patients this fundamental premise is that the process of therapy largely derives from it. The patient is taught through the Socratic method of questioning (principle 5): "(1) to become aware of what his thoughts are, (2) to examine them for cognitive distortions, (3) to substitute more balanced thoughts, and (4) to make plans to develop new thought patterns" (Beck & Emery, 1985, p. 177). Patients are taught to examine their current thoughts and test new ways of thinking on the basis of "getting the facts." Just as the development of the cognitive model of therapy is based on inductive reasoning and empirical research, in the same vein, patients are trained in a scientific way of thinking about their problems (principle 9). Patients are taught to consider beliefs as hypotheses, to conduct experiments to test their hypotheses, to pay attention to all available facts, and to revise hypotheses according to incoming data (Beck & Emery, 1985, p. 188). Cognitive therapy, therefore, uses a highly rational, empirical approach, focusing upon changing conscious thought patterns (Beck et al., 1979, p. 273; Turk et al., 1983, p. 186); there is no mention of an unconscious mind.

In contrast, an Ericksonian approach often uses trance or indirect suggestion to bypass the limitations of the conscious mind and access unconscious resources. In Ericksonian hypnotherapy trance is viewed as a context for change, and it is believed that therapeutic change can occur without conscious awareness. A fundamental difference between cognitive and Ericksonian therapies, therefore, is that cognitive therapy focuses upon and tries to change conscious thought processes, while Ericksonian therapy often attempts to access and utilize unconscious processes.

Cognitive therapy focuses on the conscious mind and uses the inductive method to generate change in conscious patterns of thinking. This is a direct approach, and from changes in cognitive functioning, changes in perceptions, behavior and affect follow. In Ericksonian hypnotherapy one often bypasses limited cognitive sets and conscious processes and utilizes the unconscious mind, which is thought to provide vast resources for change. Patients are helped to utilize their own unique life experience and associations to create and restructure themselves from within, minus the mediation of consciously directed thinking (Erickson, et al., 1976). Thus cognitive and Ericksonian therapies differ in their emphasis upon the conscious and unconscious mind.

Information Processing Model

It is of interest that, despite important differences in emphasis, the conceptualization of what treatment ultimately changes is highly similar in both cognitive and Ericksonian therapy. The goal of cognitive therapy is to change underlying cognitive schemas which guide perceptions, thinking, behavior, and affect. This notion of cognitive schemas is similar to what the Lanktons call "internal maps." With these internal maps, the individual perceives the world, interprets and acts upon information. During assessment the Lanktons ask, "Will therapy primarily work to 'edit' and alter limiting aspects of the map which seem to either prevent desired behaviors or automatically produce unpleasant feeling states and unwanted behaviors? Or will therapy work to expand and elaborate the existing map to provide new experience or behavior?" (Lankton & Lankton, 1983, p. 12). Both cognitive and Ericksonian therapy work to change these cognitive schemas or maps by which we select, interpret and act upon information.

In a previous paper, I argued that it is an information-processing model by which psychologists organize existing knowledge concerning how people perceive, process, store, and retrieve information; that such a model best explains such processes as indirect suggestion, subliminal perception, and posthypnotic suggestion; and that such a model best describes Erickson's broad-based notion of the unconscious (Feldman, 1985b). Therefore, it was with great interest that I found cognitive therapists view an information-processing model as the conceptual foundation of their school of therapy: "The main thesis [conceptually underlying cognitive therapy] is that a central process in adaptation is cognition, or information processing" (Beck & Emery, 1985, p. xv; see also Turk et al., 1983, p 344).

A brief synopsis of information-processing theory is necessary to explain the basis for this conceptual bridge between approaches. An information-processing model has traditionally involved the following stages: 1) stimulation of receptors (e.g., eyes or ears) by sensory input; 2) a stage of brief storage before becoming a conscious image; 3) a stage in which the input becomes a conscious image; 4) a stage of short-term memory; and finally, if judged to be relevant to the individual, 5) a stage in which short-term memory is rehearsed and consolidated into long-term memory. A necessity for information-processing theory is the explanation of how the wide range of channel capacity at the peripheral receptor sites is narrowed down to the relatively limited channel capacity of conscious awareness and short-term memory: "7±2" (Miller, 1956). In other words, what is the process by which an individual selects a stimulus for attention from the vast array of possibilities?

Figure 1 is a model presented by Erdelyi (1974), which illustrates the multiple stages of possible selectivity in the information processing sequence. This selectivity is generated by proposed cognitive control processes, which roughly correspond to Beck's cognitive schemas and the

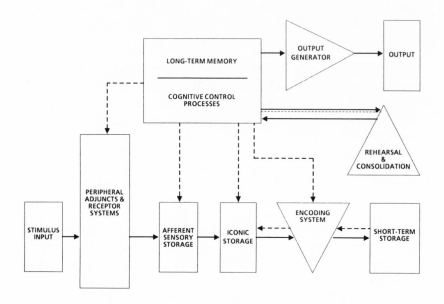

Figure 1. Erdelyi's (1974) information processing model including cognitive control processes for selection.

Lanktons' internal maps. The problem with Erdelyi's model is that it does not provide a mechanism by which information reaches these cognitive control processes so that selection can be made concerning what is to reach conscious awareness. The notion of discrimination without awareness or preconscious processing is viewed by Dixon (1981) as essential to a notion of selective attention. Hilgard (1977) agrees, stating that the mechanism for such selectivity and the "executive control and monitoring systems that permit information processing and behavior management to proceed without conscious awareness" are essential for a modern form of dissociation theory (pp. 211, 221). Finally, citing both Dixon (1981) and Bowlby (1981), Beck points out that to avoid overload in the channels responsible for the most advanced processing, which are of limited capacity, "before a person is aware of seeing or hearing a stimulus, the sensory inflow coming through his eyes or ears has already passed through many states of selection, interpretation, and appraisal" (Beck & Emery, 1985, p. 43).

To account for the fact that long-term storage or central ("executive") control processes must receive information and analyze it first at some level in order then to exert influence upon what is consciously perceived, I proposed the model illustrated in Figure 2 (Feldman, 1985b, p. 443). To indicate that in the normal perceptual process, information must be pre-

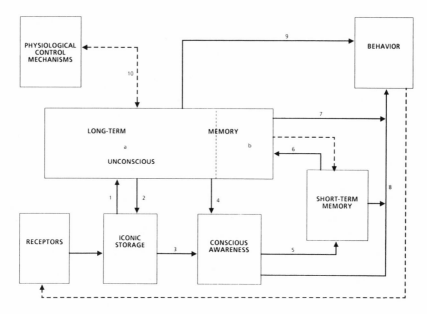

Figure 2. Feldman's (1985b) information processing model accounting for processing without awareness.

consciously processed before it reaches conscious awareness, Figure 2 has the arrows (1 & 2) in both directions between iconic storage (the most probable site of selectivity according to Erdelyi and Dixon) and long-term memory.

While one purpose of this process is to determine what is to reach the limited capacity of conscious awareness, a great deal more information is evidently processed by the nervous system than reaches conscious awareness. The research in subliminal perception (for a review see Feldman, 1985b) and the phenomenon of posthypnotic suggestion indicates that information processed without conscious awareness can also be stored in memory and affect subsequent behavior. It appears therefore that in normal states of functioning, there is a parallel processing of information, with some of the products of preconscious processing reaching awareness (arrow 3), while the rest are processed at some unconscious level. The implication is that there is a lot more to memory than has been thought. In addition to information that has reached conscious awareness, has been processed through short-term storage (arrow 5), and has been consolidated into long-term memory (arrow 6), one must postulate a parallel process (or processes). In such a process, material that bypasses awareness also reaches some kind of storage. The implication of research in subliminal perception is that the results of such processing may affect subsequent behavior in a manner qualitatively different from consciously perceived material (arrow 8 vs. arrow 9). One might view material stored through both processes (figure 2, a and b of long-term memory) that is not readily accessible as comprising the "unconscious" mind (Feldman, 1985b, p. 442).

The model's acceptance of the human capacity for parallel processing of information on multiple levels simultaneously is largely in accord with the model described by Beck. For example, to Beck anxiety involves parallel processing of information. In response to danger, a "primal response" is activated. This term is "applied to the automatic, nonconscious, nonvolitional activation of a cognitive behavioral pattern [e.g., "flight"] and also to the inhibition of a cognitive or behavioral process [e.g., "freeze"]" (Beck & Emery, 1985, p. 44). This primal response, therefore, is a rapid, unconscious response to a threat which activates a feeling of anxiety. It is a reflexive first line of defense against danger which prepares the individual for immediate action. Once the feeling of anxiety is perceived, a slower process of secondary appraisal is activated. This secondary appraisal involves an anxiety-reduction system which allows time for information processing, collecting data, evaluation and decision making. As opposed to the primal response, this is fundamentally a conscious-level process, in which the individual decides how best to evaluate the threat and how to deal with it to reduce anxiety. Thus, Beck's model fundamentally agrees that there are two parallel processes functioning simultaneously—one rapid nonconscious process by which a large amount of information is preconsciously processed and certain affective and physiological responses are activated, and a secondary, slower acting process involving conscious decision making.

I heartily agree with Beck that these two processes function in parallel and may, at times, be inconsistent in functioning. For example, more often than not during public speaking, I have felt confident on the conscious level (secondary appraisal) regarding knowing my material, having reasonably good speaking skills, and there being a generally receptive and understanding audience. Nevertheless, physiological indications of primal response arousal have usually included a dry throat, sweaty palms, and shaking hands.

In Beck's model, cognitive schemas play a central role in both the primal response and the secondary appraisal. Cognitive schemas guide an individual in terms of what to orient to in a situation and how to apply the appropriate formulas to one's analysis in preparation for response. The cognitive schemas are guided in their criteria for selection of relevant information by an adaptational principle regarding what appears to be in the individual's best interests at any one time (Beck & Emery, 1985, p. 43). This is similar to the principle of Ericksonian therapy proposed by the Lanktons: "People make the best choice for themselves at any given moment." The Lanktons further explain that, "given a person's particular frame of reference and history of learning even a 'problem' behavior or feeling is the best choice the person has learned in a particular circumstance" (1983, p. 13). In their attempts to adapt to the world, individuals develop certain cognitive sets (schemas) or internal maps with which they can more efficiently process and select information. These cognitive schemas, which in Beck's analogy are like a camera, influence the perceived picture. In the information-processing model presented in Figure 2, cognitive schemas or maps can be placed within the area of long-term memory or central processes. These schemas comprise the cognitive control mechanisms which dictate the primary response pattern to the wealth of information preconsciously processed (arrow 1), as well as selecting the information which should reach conscious awareness (arrows 2 and 3). Cognitive schemas also shape the manner in which this information will be appraised (secondary appraisal) and acted upon. That individuals generally are unaware of the nature of these cognitive schemas and that they operate outside of conscious awareness make the schemas in a sense "unconscious." In any case, it is the goal of both cognitive and Ericksonian therapies to change dysfunctional cognitive sets.

In viewing both cognitive and Ericksonian hypnotherapy from the broad perspective of the information-processing model presented in Figure 2, one can say that their seemingly fundamental differences in approach reflect differing focuses along the information-processing continuum. Cognitive therapy has focused upon the process underlying the conscious evaluation (secondary appraisal) of a situation (these processes involve arrows 2 and 3 in the model in Figure 2). Furthermore, by having individuals engage in behaviors (arrow 8) inconsistent with their appraisals, they ultimately generate change in the cognitive schemas by which the dysfunctional appraisals were made.

Cognitive therapy highlights the processes subserving conscious functioning so that individuals can learn how best to change dysfunctional appraisals and think for themselves in the future. In contrast, Ericksonian hypnotherapy uses a trance state in which the normally occurring processes subserving conscious awareness (arrow 3) are diminished. This allows a utilization of those processes which normally take place on a preconscious level (arrow 1) to be used maximally for communication to long-term storage (unconscious cognitive schemas) without conscious interference. Material can then be processed and reorganized on an unconscious level (Erickson's "unconscious search") without having to subserve conscious awareness (arrow 2). Furthermore, through limiting the ordinary information-processing channel underlying conscious awareness (arrow 3), retrieval of long-forgotten memories or unconsciously generated imagery or dreams characteristic of trance can be facilitated (arrow 4). Finally, by bypassing conscious awareness, behavioral change through posthypnotic suggestion can be generated, which then, in a manner similar to cognitive therapy, can feed back to and help change dysfunctional cognitive sets (Feldman, 1985b).

Cognitive therapy, with its focus on the conscious, and Ericksonian hypnotherapy, with its focus on the unconscious, thus represent two parts of a greater whole. This leads to the question: Why shouldn't therapists utilize the full range of available processes?

Utilizing the Strengths of Both Approaches

Obviously, my point is that the full range of processes subserving cognition or information processing should be utilized. By combining the strengths of each approach, a truly enriched comprehensive therapeutic orientation can be developed.

Cognitive therapy involves a systematic empirical approach by which assumptions and techniques are questioned and experimentally evaluated. This scientific orientation has tended to appeal to psychologists trained in research. Such an empirical approach is necessary in developing valid working maps (cognitive schemas) by which to guide clinical theory and practice (Rosenthal & Rosenthal, 1985, p. 201). The Ericksonian movement would be strengthened by greater empirical thinking. Also, the systematic approach to conceptualizing a patient's problem, developing therapeutic strategies, and testing therapeutic techniques to implement those strategies is a strength of cognitive therapy that is readily adaptable to an Ericksonian perspective.

The fundamental approach of cognitive therapy involves the utilization of the conscious mind by both the therapist and the patient. In emphasizing the novel and brilliant manner in which Erickson utilized his unconscious and the unconscious of his patients, the intelligence and persistence of Erickson's conscious mind may be forgotten. In becoming enamored of the clever and unique ways developed by Erickson for bypassing conscious awareness of intervention, the Ericksonian movement has somewhat denigrated the conscious mind. Cognitive therapy demonstrates that the conscious mind can be used to restructure the underlying schemas that guide perception, cognition, affect and behavior. Teaching coping skills and ways of thinking that can be used by patients in future situations is clearly of value. In my experience the message of "The Little Engine that

Could" was influential not only due to its trance-like indoctrination on an unconscious level, but because as a child I could consciously use the phrase "I think I can, I think I can" when faced with a challenge.

While there is much Ericksonians can learn from cognitive therapy, there are also many ways the Ericksonian movement can enrich cognitive therapy. Ericksonian therapy with its emphasis upon using the therapist's unconscious resources tends to appeal to therapists who consider themselves creative or artistic. This creative orientation can greatly expand the techniques used by cognitive therapists. Furthermore, the Ericksonian emphasis upon utilizing the vast resources of the patient's unconscious provides a greater wealth of material to use in psychotherapy. The use of language in the form of indirect suggestion can set the stage for or prime the patient for the type of changes in thinking that the cognitive therapist seeks. Cognitive therapists already use trance in teaching relaxation skills and in using imagery for training in coping skills, but they are far from maximally utilizing the trance state. There is a great wealth of hypnotic techniques which can greatly increase the power of cognitive therapy's effectiveness when an individual is in trance. These include indirect suggestions, metaphors, conscious-unconscious dissociation, embedded commands, and confusion techniques. Furthermore, since the goal is cognitive change, the tendency toward greater perceptual and cognitive flexibility, which is a part of the trance state, can be utilized.

While the cognitive therapist might question this notion of individuals being more amenable to change in a trance, the increased perceptual and cognitive flexibility can be explained as well by the information-processing model. One's cognitive schemas develop as a means of processing and organizing input from the outside world. They are therefore embedded in the conscious, reality-testing mind and its function of adapting to the external world. If one changes this state of awareness by minimizing or confusing external input, as in a trance induction, these reality-testing schemas are deactivated. An internal search therefore ensues (Erickson's "unconscious search") in an attempt to adapt to this altered state. One can therefore view trance as a state in which an individual is more amenable to change because cognitive structures tied to the external world are deactivated and the individual is in a state of searching for new structures relevant to this altered reality. The individual is therefore internally searching for relevant experience and resources to utilize as well as probably being more open to external suggestions.

In attempting to develop a comprehensive therapeutic viewpoint, one might sensibly ask: When is it best to use primarily a cognitive therapy orientation and when to use primarily an Ericksonian orientation? Once again, the information-processing model provides at least a partial an-

swer. If the symptoms in question appear to involve primarily unconscious processing as characterized by the primal response pattern (described by Beck), hypnosis or work on an unconscious level seems indicated. In contrast, if the symptoms involve the secondary appraisal
mechanisms underlying conscious reality testing, a cognitive approach
might be warranted. Also, if symptoms involve cognitive or behavioral
skills deficits, a lack of information or presence of misinformation impair-
ing the development of adaptive cognitive schemas, a more direct approach seems warranted. Fundamentally, the therapist should evaluate
whether the symptoms are activated by unconscious processes, for which
hypnosis can be useful, or involve thoughts and behaviors under conscious control, which might be changed by cognitive therapeutic or
Ericksonian strategic approaches (a similar diagnostic dichotomy was
suggested by O'Hanlon in a workshop presentation, May 4, 1986, New
York City).

In summary, both cognitive and Ericksonian psychotherapy provide a
wide range of therapeutic strategies and techniques. Seemingly fundamental differences in these approaches can be seen as reflecting different
emphases along an information-processing continuum. One can utilize
both conscious and unconscious processes in effecting change in underlying cognitive schemas or maps which guide perception, thinking, behavior and affect. This utilization of the entire person seems to be most in
accord with the way Erickson lived and worked.

References

Beck, A. J., & Emery, G. (1985). *Anxiety disorders and phobias: A cognitive perspective.*
    New York: Basic Books.
Beck, A. J., Rush, A. J., Shaw, Jr., & Emery, G. (1979). *Cognitive therapy of depression.*
    New York: Guilford.
Bowlby, J. (1981). Cognitive processes in the genesis of psychopathology. Invited
    address to the Biannual Meeting of the Society for Research in Child Develop-
    ment, Boston, April 1981.
Dixon, N. F. (1981). *Preconscious processing.* New York: Wiley.
Erdelyi, M. H. (1974). A new look at the "new look": Perceptual defense and
    vigilance. *Psychological Review, 81,* 1–25.
Erickson, M. H., Rossi, E. T., & Rossi, I. (1976). *Hypnotic realities: The induction of
    clinical hypnosis and forms of indirect suggestion.* New York: Irvington.
Feldman, J. (1985a). The work of Milton Erickson: A multisystem model of eclectic
    therapy. *Psychotherapy: Theory, Research and Practice, 22,* 154–162
Feldman, J. (1985b). Subliminal perception and information processing theory:
    Empirical and conceptual validation of Erickson's notion of the unconscious.
    In J. Zeig (Ed.), *Ericksonian psychotherapy, Volume I: Structures* (pp. 431–447).
    New York: Brunner/Mazel.
Gordon, D., & Myers-Anderson, M. (1981). *Phoenix: Therapeutic patterns of Milton
    Erickson.* Cupertino, CA: Meta.

Grodner, B. (1986). Learning Erickson's methods. In B. Zilbergeld, M. Edelstein, & D. Araoz (Eds.), *Hypnosis: Questions and answers*. New York: Norton.

Hilgard, E. R. (1977). *Divided consciousness*. New York: Wiley.

Lankton, S., & Lankton, C. (1983). *The answer within: A clinical framework of Ericksonian hypnotherapy*. New York: Brunner/Mazel.

Miller, G. A. (1956). The magical number seven, plus or minus two: Some limits on our capacity for processing information. *Psychology Review, 63*, 81–97.

O'Hanlon, B. (1985). A study guide of frameworks of Milton Erickson's hypnosis and therapy. In J. Zeig (Ed.), *Ericksonian psychotherapy, Volume I: Structures* (pp. 33–51). New York: Brunner/Mazel.

Rosen, S. (1982). *My voice will go with you: The teaching tales of Milton H. Erickson*. New York: Norton.

Rosenthal, J. T., & Rosenthal, R. H. (1985). Clinical stress management. In D. H. Barlow (Ed.), *Clinical handbook of psychological disorders* (pp. 145–205). New York: Guilford.

Turk, D. C., Meichenbaum, D., & Genest, M. (1983). *Pain and behavioral medicine: A cognitive-behavioral perspective*. New York: Guilford.

Zeig, J. (Ed.) (1982). *Ericksonian approaches to hypnosis and psychotherapy*. New York: Brunner/Mazel.

Zeig, J. (1986). Motivating patients to follow prescriptions. In B. Zilbergeld, M. G. Edelstein & D. J. Araoz (Eds.), *Hypnosis: questions and answers* (pp. 252–254). New York: Norton.

Changing Early Life Decisions Using Ericksonian Hypnosis

Maggie Phillips, Ph.D.

Maggie Phillips, Ph.D. (Fielding Institute) is in private practice and consultation in Oakland, California, and on the teaching faculty of the California Institute of Clinical Hypnosis.

Phillips provides an excellent summary of the Redecision Therapy of Robert and Mary Goulding and illustrates how Ericksonian goals and methods compare and contrast. She demonstrates how Ericksonian techniques can be used in the practice of Redecision Therapy to enrich and enhance each stage of work.

Introduction

The redecision model of psychotherapy developed by Robert and Mary Goulding has received widespread recognition as an effective way of identifying and changing decisions, made in response to early parental messages, which no longer work in the individual's current life. Redecision therapy attempts to uncover early, dysfunctional decisions, examine their emotional and cognitive structure, and facilitate a redecision.

This chapter demonstrates how techniques of Ericksonian therapy are especially suited to enhance redecision therapy by offering numerous options for clinicians at each stage of the redecision process. First, an overview of redecision and Ericksonian therapies is presented, with emphasis on comparative therapeutic assumptions, goals, tasks, and techniques. Next, suggestions are made for matching specific Ericksonian options with the four basic stages or redecision therapy, using clinical case examples. Finally, conclusions are drawn about the effectiveness of Ericksonian approaches in strengthening and expanding the redecision model.

Address reprint requests to Maggie Phillips, Ph.D., 1334 El Centro Avenue, Oakland, CA 94602.

Overview and Comparison

Redecision therapy was developed as a way of integrating the clearly defined theory of transactional analysis (TA) and the powerful emotion-evoking techniques of gestalt therapy. The focus of this approach is to identify "the injunction-decision complex" (Goulding & Goulding, 1979, p. 42). Injunctions are negative messages given directly or indirectly to the child from parents with unresolved painful experiences from their own early life. The Gouldings' list of injunctions includes: "Don't. Don't be. Don't be close. Don't be important. Don't be a child. Don't grow. Don't succeed. Don't be you. Don't be sane. Don't be well. Don't belong" (Goulding & Goulding, 1979, p. 35).

From a redecision perspective, the child has the ability to accept or reject these parental messages; if accepted, the child's responses may take the form of a decision. For example, if a child receives and accepts the message "Don't succeed," possible decisions might be "I'm stupid," "I can't do anything right," or "I'll show you I can succeed if it kills me." The Gouldings also believe that in some cases, injunctions are not given by the parent but by the child, who is capable of fantasizing, distorting, and inventing parental messages. For instance, if a parent dies unexpectedly, the child may decide never to be close again to avoid reexperiencing such a painful loss. Similarly, the child might give herself a "don't be" injunction, deciding that her disaffiliative behavior (magically) caused the death and therefore she does not deserve to go on living. These injunctions, and the resulting decisions, may occur regardless of actual parental messages at the time of the event.

The process of redecision therapy usually begins with a current adult problem identified by the client. The redecision therapist obtains recent examples of the difficulty, and helps the client reenact a current problem scene, using gestalt role-play. During the reenactment, dysfunctional thoughts, feelings, and behaviors become recognizable and the therapist assists in uncovering the original parental injunction(s) and child decisions.

The scene of each early decision is then reenacted with the client in the Child ego state. According to TA theory, the early Child ego state is similar to the id, which consists of primitive drives, and preverbal or symbolic experiences. This state seems closer to the psychoanalytic concept of the unconscious mind than to Ericksonian concepts. An aspect of the early Child referred to as the adaptive Child acts to accept or reject parental messages, overruling the free or natural Child for survival purposes. In redecision therapy, the third and last aspect, the early Adult in the Child, makes a new decision, based on new information, to override the pathological adaption and function more freely (Goulding & Goulding, 1979, p. 19).

Following what is usually a brief (20 minutes) piece of redecision work, the client is invited to practice and reinforce the redecision within the group therapy milieu, and thereafter in everyday life.

At first glance, Ericksonian hypnotherapy appears quite different from redecision therapy. While the Gouldings emphasize conscious awareness and responsibility for change, Erickson focused on unconscious processes and learning beyond conscious control. While redecision therapists orchestrate change by promoting direct understanding of dysfunctional beliefs, emotional responses and behaviors and subsequent direct practice of new decisions, Ericksonian therapists usually provoke change through indirect suggestion, paradoxical directives, utilization of client's dysfunctional behavior, and creation of different sensory, cognitive, and emotional experiences.

Despite these differences, however, there are important similarities in the two approaches which make possible the notion of effective integration of Ericksonian principles with the redecision model. A discussion follows of parallels between the two therapies, as well as those departure points where Ericksonian perspectives might offer ways of strengthening and expanding the way in which the redecision model is currently practiced.

Therapeutic Goals

Redecision and Ericksonian therapies both have as a central goal the facilitation of change in clients through new learning. The Gouldings believe that emotions are highly sensitive to learning influences during various stages of development, and that dysfunctional learning experiences become embedded in an individual's basic strategies for living (Madison, 1985, p. 21). Through redecision work, clients learn how they have come to make dysfunctional decisions, and that they have the power to decide differently in the here and now.

Ericksonian therapy is also committed to concept of change through new learning. Erickson's use of a learning framework applied to every level of therapy; he referred to the global task of learning to adjust better to everyday life as well as to the more precise task of helping an individual learn through subtle unconscious movement in a trance state (Lankton & Lankton, 1983, p. 149).

Like the Gouldings, Erickson also believed that early learning plays an important part in later life difficulties. Much as redecision therapy seeks to uncover dysfunctional emotional responses and decisions to early negative parental messages, Ericksonian therapy often attempts to identify and bridge gaps in an individual's learning history and psychosocial development.

One of Erickson's best known case examples involving early learning is the February Man. He used hypnotic age regression and a metaphorical approach with a pregnant young woman who was doubtful of her own abilities to have and raise children. In a series of age regressions, Erickson visited her in trance at various stages of childhood, metaphorically identifying himself as the February Man—a friend of her father. By providing important nurturing experiences that the woman had missed as a little girl, Erickson was able to help his client develop a new sense of confidence and to "redecide" that she could deliver and raise her first child successfully and happily.

Both redecision and Ericksonian therapies emphasize an interpersonal context. The Gouldings' focus on the "injunction-decision" complex provides an interpersonal framework which describes the interactive contributions of both parent and child that can result in dysfunctional patterns. Gestalt reenactments of both early and current scenes emphasize relationships between parents and child, as well as among other significant people in the client's current and past life. Each contact offers an opportunity to change relevant but faulty interpersonal patterns.

Erickson also stressed the importance of interpersonal dynamics in treatment interventions. He would often involve parents, spouse, siblings, roommates, or employers in the therapy. For example, in a case of a young woman who vomited whenever she dated and who would not talk with anyone about this difficulty, Erickson arranged for her roommate to be the identified patient. He worked with the real client indirectly by inviting her to be a part of her roommate's therapy. Asking her to pay attention to her roommate's hypnotic experiences, he embedded many indirect suggestions for her benefit. This led to her willingness to seek therapy openly in the second session. By considering the resources as well as the limitations of the client's social network, Erickson could facilitate necessary interpersonal learning.

As I have shown, the redecision and Ericksonian approaches have similar therapeutic goals of promoting change through new learning, correcting inadequate or distorted past learning experiences relevant to current dysfunctions, and utilizing an interpersonal context for change. However, Ericksonian therapy makes several important departures from the redecision model.

First, in contrast to the Gouldings, Erickson believed that the most important learning occurred at the unconscious level. While redecision therapy stresses conscious awareness and responsibility for change,

Erickson invited clients to surrender conscious involvement for learning and allow the unconscious mind to direct and integrate the necessary learning for change:

> Your unconscious can try anything it wishes but your conscious mind isn't going to do anything of importance....There is nothing really important except the activity of your unconscious mind. And that can be whatever your unconscious mind desires....And in the trance state you can let your mind survey that vast store of learning that you...have achieved without knowing it. And many of the learnings that were important to you consciously have slipped into your unconscious mind. (Erickson, Rossi & Rossi, 1976, pp. 9–11)

Second, because of his focus on the unconscious, Erickson encouraged change through learning on multiple levels of awareness. The Gouldings, using a variety of techniques, including fantasy, imagery, and desensitization, which access and resolve experiences on a symbolic or less conscious level, focus this material primarily back to the conscious level. Contrary to Erickson, they offer a conscious framework for the client to claim and practice responsibility for this new learning.

Erickson differentiated between unconscious and conscious levels of awareness and believed that "one of the greatest advantages of hypnotherapy lies in the opportunity to work independently with the unconscious without being hampered by the reluctance, or sometimes actual inability, of the conscious mind to accept therapeutic gains" (Erickson, 1980, p. 40). A major goal of Ericksonian therapy is to help the client move away from the habitual and often restrictive patterns of the conscious mind to the more intuitive, diffuse and spontaneous learning patterns of the unconscious mind. Though the Ericksonian therapist often helps the client integrate learnings on a conscious level, just as often the client is left with the suggestion that this integration will occur unconsciously when the time is right.

A third departure of Ericksonian therapy from the redecision model is in the area of therapeutic goals. Where the Gouldings' goal is to promote direct understanding of learning, Erickson often deliberately pursued an indirect route. Believing in the importance of unconscious learning, and promoting change at multiple levels of awareness, he emphasized the use of *indirect* strategies that bypassed conscious understanding. He perceived the conscious mind to be the less reliable, more limited, and most resistive aspect of mental activity; therefore, he attempted to move beyond an individual's learned limitations in order to better facilitate unconscious processes. By comparison, redecision therapy confronts resistance to change directly by clarifying and challenging different types of "impasses." Ericksonian therapy attempts to create through indirection an extensive, positive set of learning experiences at the unconscious level which will circumvent objections of the conscious mind:

> By such...indirect suggestion the patient is enabled to go through those difficult inner processes of disorganization, reorganization, reassociating and projection of inner experience to meet the requirements of [therapeutic goals]. (Erickson, 1980, p. 1)

Thus, Erickson's use of indirection provides a sharp contrast to the redecision model's focus on direct, conscious access to the client's inner experiences and resources available for change.

Therapeutic Tasks and Assumptions

The second focus of comparison between the two approaches is the area of therapeutic assumptions. One of the major assumptions made by the redecision therapist is that clients have choices about how they think, feel, and act. The Gouldings usually promote this idea of choice from their opening interactions with clients as they ask, "What are you *choosing* to change about yourself today?"

Based on this belief, the major task of the redecision therapist is to help clients move from general desires to a statement of specific goals for change, usually formulated in behavioral terms. For example, in working with a client who says, "I want to fulfill myself and own myself," the therapist clarifies and explores, often asking for specific, current examples of what the client means:

Cl: I want to fulfill myself and own myself.
Th: Say that in kid language.
Cl: I always have this feeling that something is wrong with me.
Th: Yeah, like what?
Cl: That I'm dumb and nasty and that I don't like people.
Th: Are you all those things?
Cl: No, I am not. That's it. I want to stop all this downing of myself.
(Goulding & Goulding, 1979, p. 53)

Like redecision therapists, Ericksonian therapists also share the important and basic assumption that clients have the power of choice about their lives. Therapy is established in such a way that clients can maximize their ability to choose to enhance rather than limit this autonomy. Yet Erickson had a very different notion about how clients' power of choice would best be served:

> When you understand how man really defends his intellectual ideas and how emotional he gets about it, you should realize that the first thing in psychotherapy is not to try to compel him to change his ideation; rather you go along with it and change it in a gradual fashion and create situations wherein he himself willingly changes his thinking. (Erickson, 1980, p. 335)

In contrast to redecision therapy, the task of the Ericksonian therapist is to accept and utilize clients' current ideas about themselves and what they need to change, and to gradually teach clients new possibilities in such a way that they willingly choose these new options. Ericksonian therapists help clients move from more specific, often restrictive concepts of change to more global, comprehensive understandings of what is possible to experience.

Often, clients want help in eliminating a choice. While redecision therapists might support such a change (e.g., eliminating negative self-critical statements), Ericksonian therapists often assume that the client will automatically make the best choice once it is available, and may leave the old choice still available in the event that it becomes the "best choice" in some future situation. Thus, a primary task of the Ericksonian therapist is to *expand*, rather than narrow, the client's field of choice, in order to add behaviors, thoughts and feelings that may have been previously unavailable.

Therapeutic Techniques

In addition to important similarities and differences in the areas of therapeutic goals, tasks, and assumptions, redecision and Ericksonian therapies also can be compared in terms of therapeutic techniques.

When therapists are trained in the redecision model, they are taught a structured process with specific techniques, which they learn in highly focused practice sessions. When beginning work with clients, in order to clarify initial contracts, redecision therapists are taught to confront ways that clients abdicate responsibility for their own choices, and to question words that are vague or indicate a lack of commitment (e.g., "I'll try to"; "I'd like to be able to"; "I think I might want to"). At this point in the process, the therapist is active and directive with the client, asking such questions as: "What are you saying to yourself that you are willing to stop saying? In what circumstances did you learn to think, feel, and act that way?" (Pulleyblank & McCormick, 1985, p. 53).

Once the therapeutic contract is agreed upon, the redecision therapist uses a number of techniques to help the client access and reenact scenes from the recent past as well as those from early childhood. The therapist may simply give the client a direct suggestion to choose a recent (or past) scene when she was feeling, thinking or behaving in ways related to changes she wants to make. If more help is needed, the therapist may ask the client to close her eyes and recall a certain scene from memory, or even to imagine such a scene. Once scenes are accessed, gestalt or psychodrama role-playing techniques are used to help the client reexperience the event directly, or more indirectly fantasize the scene. During these reenactments, or role-plays, the redecision therapist assists the client in maintaining cathexis of the Child ego state through such strategies as encouraging the use of "little kid" language, expressing experiences in emotional terms, or describing aspects of the child self in a particular scene (e.g., How tall were you? What are you wearing?).

At the redecision stage, the therapist points out directly parental messages and the resulting decisions about self and others. Here, the language of transactional analysis is used (e.g., ego states, injunctions), and if unfamiliar, is taught to clients, with specific and relevant examples. Clients are helped to experience the emotional consequences of the early decision from the Child ego state and, while using a rational understanding that it is possible to choose differently now, change their response and decisions about themselves. Again, this is conducted in the role-play enactment with direct suggestions from the therapist.

After the redecision, clients are directed by the therapist to practice the new decision by changing real transactions in their daily life. Assignments are usually carefully structured, and progress is carefully monitored by both therapist and clients; the result is behavioral changes that have been specified in the original therapy contract.

In contrast to the relative clarity of the redecision approach, Ericksonian techniques appear to be complex and unwieldy. Those who have studied Erickson's work have used widely different terminology to describe his treatment interventions. Erickson's own statements about his strategies, even with careful editing, often seem to take on the qualities of the unconscious mind itself and can appear diffuse and challenging to replicate.

Although Erickson used direct suggestion and gave many directives to his clients, he is best known for the indirect approach in reaching and stimulating the unconscious mind. Lankton and Lankton (1983) categorize major features of the Ericksonian approach in this way:

1) indirection—the use of indirect suggestion, binds, metaphor, and resource retrieval;

2) conscious/unconscious dissociation—multiple level communication, interspersal, double binds, multiple embedded metaphors;
and,

3) utilization of the client's behavior—paradox, behavioral matching, naturalistic induction, symptom prescription, and strategic
use of trance phenomena. (p. 6)

These techniques are used in Ericksonian therapy at every stage of
work, from forming an initial alliance with the client and accessing unconscious resources and experiences, to establishing new, effective learning
sets for change and integrating that change into different levels of awareness and usefulness. Different from the highly structured redecision approach, Ericksonian therapists apply these techniques with flexibility, attempting to introduce interventions in sequences matching each client's
special needs and level of responsiveness.

Instead of confrontation, Ericksonian therapists demonstrate acceptance of the clients' symptoms. They often begin work by paradoxically
directing clients to perform in the same dysfunctional ways, while reframing or changing the context of the symptom.

Rather than teaching specific guidelines or language to clients,
Ericksonian therapists attempt to have clients discover their own solutions. By using such strategies as deliberately vague language with multiple meanings, implied suggestions, and metaphorical references, clients
can, through an internal search, select their own "best" associations and
responses. This approach appreciates that many important associations
may often be outside of conscious awareness.

Stages of Redecision and Ericksonian Options

The above comparisons between redecision and Ericksonian approaches indicate that although these therapies share many of the same
goals and assumptions, tasks of the therapist and therapeutic techniques
reflect very different paths of implementation. The primary premise of this
paper is that the differences found in Ericksonian therapy offer important
options that can strengthen and enhance redecision work by providing a
focus on more unconscious levels of experience. Suggestions are presented
for applying Ericksonian options to four major stages of redecision therapy: contracting, identifying and experiencing early decision, making the
redecision, and integrating the redecision.

Contracting

The therapist's focus at this stage of redecision therapy is to obtain a
specific, behavioral contract about what clients are willing and ready to

change. Many clients, however, do not really know what they need to change in order to relieve the symptoms they are experiencing; others make a compliant contract to be a "good client"; still others present "resistances" such as not believing change is possible. For these and other individuals for whom direct, behavioral contracts are not effective, the more indirect Ericksonian approaches, which accept whatever attitudes and behaviors the client presents and which can begin to foster new awareness and learning at an unconscious level, can be a viable alternative.

As an Ericksonian/redecision therapist, I have worked with many such clients who have responded to this integrated approach. For example, in interviewing a young man enrolled in a university agriculture program, who had been treated for symptoms of depression without success by several psychiatrists and therapists and who expressed serious doubts about my being able to help him, I began to talk about his lack of energy and hopelessness as a time when:

> Your energy fields have been lying fallow for too long and it must seem to you as if the fruits of your labors have been rotting and wasting away. It's at times like these that farmers feel like giving up their life's work, but what they have no way of knowing is that that is the very time when it's most propitious for them to plant a new crop...since their motivation is strong enough then to help them find that last shred of strength to dig down deep enough to get to the roots of the problem.

After I presented several metaphors which seemed to match his present and past experiences, he began responding with more positive statements and was able to make a therapy contract, which in subsequent sessions was carried out effectively.

Other helpful Ericksonian strategies at this stage might include: reframing the client's presenting difficulties in more acceptable terms; the use of conscious-unconscious dissociation to teach the concept that meaningful learning occurs at many unconscious levels and that this approach to the problem will be effective because it will utilize unconscious possibilities and resources unavailable to the client before now; interspersal and indirect suggestion to plant positive "seeds" that can generate a positive learning set for current and subsequent therapy sessions.

Although the redecision therapist may want to obtain an explicit behavioral contract, an important option to consider is an unconscious contract—an implicit, open-ended contract acknowledging that an infinite number of changes are possible, unknown both to therapist and client, and that the client will select those that best meet her of his needs at every level of experience as new learning gradually occurs. Such diversity at the contracting stage does not sacrifice need specificity but rather may help clients begin their thinking in fruitful areas, while showing acceptance for them in their new therapy undertaking.

Identifying and Experiencing Early Decision

During the second stage of redecision, the therapist's focus is to help uncover the early decision which is seen as the impetus for the client's current life difficulties. Redecision therapists begin by helping clients recall a recent scene when problem responses occurred, then direct clients to reenact the dialogue between themselves and significant others. The goal at this point is to help clients experience feelings that surface from the Child ego state rather than to achieve rational understanding.

The Ericksonian approach offers options for this stage which might include using other types of directives, such as paradox, binds, and symptom prescription. In the case example of the depressed client, I instructed him at this stage:

> Really let yourself experience right now some of those awful, depressed feelings you've been telling me about...and don't let them slip away too quickly...because there are some things those feelings can teach you through your unconscious mind...things you can't learn any other way. And do you really want to miss out on *any* important learning for yourself?

This kind of directive permits clients to have the problem feelings in a context in which they can be understood to be useful.

Another possible option is to help clients reexperience a problem in a trance state as a way of accessing unconscious and conscious responses to the interaction. Suggestions directed to all the senses can be given to promote a more complete experience. For example, I might utilize observable responses to present a naturalistic induction to the depressed client cited above:

> Noticing the movements of your eyes and the way your hands seem to turn over that notion right now...maybe just as you discover the beginnings of those feelings...you can close your eyes so comfortably...and just let your mind drift back to that time you can recall when those feelings seem so real...

The second phase of work at this stage involves bridging from the current problem to the earlier childhood (decision) scene. Redecision therapists usually give a direct suggestion that clients "go back to a time when you remember first learning to feel that way"; if clients have difficulty recalling an actual scene, they are encouraged to imagine such a scene. Again, the goal is to help clients experience feelings that surface in the early scene and to determine, "What did you decide about yourself? Your father/mother?" Once decisions are identified, their relevance is discussed in terms of subsequent reactions, including those in the current problem scene explored in phase one of this stage. Here the goal is rational, adult awareness and insight.

Ericksonian options include using additional accessing and recall strategies that can help clients reexperience early scenes more completely. For example, the thoughtful use of age regression suggestions can elicit deeper Child responses, and facilitate the internal search for a pivotal experience central to the decision. Deeper, less conscious access to this material can also be achieved by the use of trance, incorporating nonverbal and symbolic experiences of self into the internal search.

Making Redecisions

The third major stage involves replaying the early scene and changing emotional and verbal responses to construct a new decision. The redecision therapist is active in helping clients reexperience early scenes with adult knowledge and other parts of themselves that were not available in the original experience. Through such directives as, "Now tell your mother how you really feel about how she attended to your brother's needs while ignoring yours," clients discover new, more effective ways of being in the early scene, and in the process of discovery, make new decisions about organizing their experience and conducting their life.

Ericksonian options for this stage can include the use of techniques such as age regression and dissociation to review events and to facilitate more involved reentry into the early scene with additional unconscious and conscious resources. Sample age regression suggestions might include:

Going back to that time and place with new understandings can take so many different forms...like a big hand strong enough to hold your little one securely.

Dissociative review allows clients who are particularly fearful of reentering a painful or traumatic scene to review the scene from a safe and comfortable distance. Erickson used this technique in the Monde case:

In other words, would you like to see your adult body sitting in that chair over there? And your unconscious mind over here, but your body's over there? (Lustig, 1975)

The new decision may be made effective by the use of either conscious or unconscious processes, depending on such factors as the client's ease of response to hypnosis, extent of amnesia for trance experiences, and expressed desire for conscious understanding.

Integrating New Decisions

During the final stage of redecision, therapists assign clients ways of practicing their new decision about themselves and related patterns of interpersonal responding, including new ways of reinforcing, validating, or "stroking" self and others. Generally, this practice occurs outside of the work between client and therapist.

Several Ericksonian techniques, including assignments and homework rehearsal, if used during this stage, aid integration and future learning. Age progression, for example, provides an opportunity for clients to imagine themselves at some future time when the new decision has been fully integrated.

Suggestions can be given for the use of visual, kinesthetic and auditory experiences to make the scene more real. Posthypnotic suggestion is useful in pacing the gradual integration of the new decision and associated new behaviors, thoughts, and feelings, beginning in the trance state and continuing at the client's own pace over a period of weeks, months, and even years. Key words, or cues can be included as reinforcers:

Each time you walk across a new threshold, you can be reminded of that glimpse of yourself that is appearing more and more real...the you that is the product of such important new decisions and experiences.

Finally, self-image building (Lankton & Lankton, 1983, p. 318) or visual rehearsal can be used to help clients develop and appreciate new parts of themselves that are necessary to integrate the new changes fully into every aspect of their life.

Conclusions

Redecision therapy is a clear, direct model of change. It is highly effective in promoting change through a brief model using structured techniques that are easily taught and replicated. Ericksonian therapy shares many of the same goals and some of the same assumptions, but helps clients change through more indirect avenues which incorporate the involvement of unconscious learning and resources.

This chapter has given suggestions for the use of Ericksonian principles and techniques as options for therapists at each of the four major stages of redecision therapy. Ericksonian approaches of indirection, dissociation, and utilization are uniquely suited to enrich redecision therapy. Because Ericksonian approaches excel in retrieving resources and expanding choices in approaching and reaching therapeutic goals, it may be valuable also to consider how to integrate them into other therapies.

References

Erickson, M. H. (1980). Innovative hypnotherapy. In E. L. Rossi (Ed.), *The collected papers of Milton H. Erickson* (Vol. 4). New York: Irvington.

Erickson, M. H., Rossi, E. L., & Rossi, S. (1976). *Hypnotic realities*. New York: Irvington.

Goulding, M., & Goulding, R. (1979). *Changing lives through redecision therapy*. New York: Brunner/Mazel.

Lankton, S., & Lankton, C, (1983). *The answer within: A clinical framework of Ericksonian hypnotherapy*. New York: Brunner/Mazel.

Lustig, H. S. (1975). *The artistry of Milton H. Erickson, M.D.* (a videotape). Haverford, PA: Herbert S. Lustig, M.D., Ltd.

Madison, P. (1985). *Redecision* therapy: What it is, how and why it works. In L. B. Kadis (Ed.), *Redecision therapy: Expanded perspectives* (pp. 20–25). Watsonville, CA: Western Institute for Group and Family Therapy.

Pulleyblank, E., & McCormick, P. (1985). The stages of redecision therapy. In L. B. Kadis (Ed.), *Redecision therapy: Expanded perspectives* (pp. 51–57). Watsonville, CA: Western Institute for Group and Family Therapy.

Medical
Applications

The Application of Ericksonian Principles to the Use of Medication

Steven Goldsmith, M.D.

Steven Goldsmith, M.D. (Columbia College of Physicians and Surgeons) is Attending Physician in the Department of Psychiatry at Burbank Hospital in Fitchburg, Massachusetts, and Clinical Instructor in Psychiatry at Boston University School of Medicine. He is author of The Trance State: Varieties of the Healing Experience *(Irvington) and* The Psychotherapy of People with Physical Symptoms: Brief Strategic Approaches *(University Press of America).*

Goldsmith presents case examples from his psychiatric practice, which support his observations that an indirect approach including paradoxical directives is facilitative with patients who attribute symbolic, psychological and interpersonal significance to the use of prescription medicine. Goldsmith reminds us that the use of medication is not antithetical to an Ericksonian approach. Rather, medication and the way that it is prescribed can foster strategic goals.

Psychotropic, or mind-altering, medication is widely used in a variety of therapeutic contexts. Psychotherapists, patients and families often have strong feelings and opinions regarding these drugs, and the management of their use is frequently complex. The systemic influences that surround the prescription and use or misuse of psychotropic medication would be well-addressed by Erickson's utilization approach. However, the strategic management of medicine-related behaviors has rarely been discussed in the literature.

The prescription of medication can affect important interpersonal transactions within a family and other systems impinging upon a patient. In addition, prescriptions can represent the main currency of an important relationship a patient already has with a physician. The use of medication is a principal way physicians feel they help others, and the most frequent means by which patients hope for relief. The very issues associated with the prescription and management of psychotropic medication create critical opportunities for diagnosis and treatment. The purpose of this chapter

---

Address reprint requests to Steven Goldsmith, M.D., 44 Bond Street, Fitchburg, MA 01420.

is: 1) to delineate a role for medication as an element in strategic interventions designed to address broader patient issues; 2) to illustrate applications of Ericksonian principles to increase patient compliance in taking prescribed medication; and 3) to discuss the use of patient responses to medication as a diagnostic tool.

Erickson's work emphasizes the importance of meeting patients and their associates within their models of the world. It stresses the related importance of utilizing, rather than ignoring or arbitrarily confronting, existing attitudes and behaviors that become evident during treatment. Any occurrences during the course of therapy, including patient behaviors and family interactions around the use of medication, can potentially be incorporated into an Ericksonian approach. On the other hand, any issue of importance to the patient system that remains unaddressed or unacknowledged by the therapist may serve as a nucleus for resistance or can be used to sabotage treatment. All of the above suggests that the intentional or unwitting exclusion of the area of medication from strategic consideration during treatment planning may be a serious oversight.

Medications can have a variety of meanings for patients. They can be the mother's milk that nurtures and protects them, their safety blanket in the dark, their refuge in the storm, the humiliating evidence that they cannot take care of themselves, a dreaded symbol of dependency, a potential or real poison, a means of self-abuse, a means of malevolent coercion or intrusion, or the well-meant but futile offering of a physician no more able to help them than anyone else has been. Medications can be triangulated into relationships so that couples talk about or argue over the medicines instead of dealing with more intimate matters between themselves. Medications can be the coin of hostile, overprotective relationships in which one person controls them for or administers them to another.

When patients are prescribed beneficial medications and take them as instructed over time, it can be sufficient for the prescriber and/or therapist to assume a straightforward attitude with the patient: "You should take this medication." There is no reason to use paradoxical or elegant, indirect interventions with a patient who complies with simple directions. This is as true of directives and recommendations regarding medication as it is of interventions about anything else. Nondirect approaches become useful when a patient or the patient's family is likely not to comply with medications that are essential to treatment.

Case 1

In my role as a medication consultant at a mental health center, I was asked to see Harold, a 36-year-old man who was in therapy with a clinician there. This patient was dependent on his parents, who controlled and administered his medications, which were prescribed for severe anxiety. The patient and his family placed more importance on his medications than on any other issue affecting them and frequently badgered the agency staff to alter his medications. At the time of the consultation, the patient was receiving the tranquilizer, Xanax, the latest in an exhaustive series of medications found ineffective for him.

I told the three of them that, although I did not feel that *any* medications would significantly help the patient—certainly not as much as psychotherapy would—I would be willing to prescribe Xanax because his parents' administering it to him served as an important reminder of how his anxiety helped maintain the family togetherness and allowed his parents to feel needed; without that, they would be faced with their fears of growing old together in their postretirement life. I predicted serious distress for both parents if reminders of the patient's problem disappeared too quickly. I informed them that I would, therefore, continue prescribing Xanax in order to spare them that even worse distress. These interventions of reframing, prediction of failure, restraint from change, and symptom prescription were accepted by the family with bewilderment and annoyance. Subsequently, however, they focused much less on medications and more on family issues in the treatment.

I would like to use several other cases to illustrate an indirect approach for various patient needs.

Case 2

Jill was a 55-year-old woman with a bipolar disorder who remained free of life-threatening psychotic episodes only while taking lithium. She repeatedly expressed interest in seeing how she would fare without the medication. If I didn't immediately agree to take her off the lithium, she angrily got up to leave. She accepted and complied with my prescriptions only when I told her she might have a good point and that it *would* be interesting to see how she did without medication. This scenario was repeated numerous times while she remained compliant with the lithium prescriptions.

Case 3

Paulette was a 50-year-old woman with a bipolar disorder who had a history of rejection of treatment and noncompliance with lithium and Haldol, medications that had previously proven valuable to her in aborting severe manic episodes. She was also taking iron pills that her internist felt were unnecessary. As I began to follow her case, she became more and more opposed to continuing the lithium and Haldol, particularly when I discussed these medications with her.

Over time, even though I continued to prescribe these two medications, I began to talk with her more about the iron pills and to emphasize strongly to her that she needed to continue taking *them*. She eventually stopped her iron pills, but became fully compliant with the prescriptions of the other two medications. The focus of opposition onto the iron and away from her psychotropic medications continued for a couple of years—an uncharacteristically long period of compliance for her—until she moved to another region to live with a relative and was lost to follow-up.

In this case, resistance to medication was discharged in a focused fashion so that the most important treatment goals were not jeopardized. Similarly, Erickson demonstrated that a hypnotist can employ certain emotionally loaded words as "lightning rods" for the patient's anxiety, hostility, or opposition so that the patient takes issue with these words rather than with the therapeutic process as a whole.

Case 4

In addition to other interventions, I have repeatedly found "one down" positioning to be helpful with patients who request medication, decline to express their own wishes, leave everything up to the doctor, then render the medication ineffective by means of noncompliance, side effects, or unchanged symptomatology. These individuals could be labeled "help-rejecting complainers."

An example was Martha, a 32-year-old woman, chronically and markedly depressed, who had previously received numerous medications that had caused intolerable side effects or that she felt were ineffective. When I first saw her she was taking the antidepressant Elavil in an erratic and sometimes self-abusive fashion. Martha's lifestyle was characterized by total dependence on physicians and no independent interests. She proclaimed to me that she needed medication, but that she was only a "dumb patient" who needed to be told what to do with her medication.

I informed her that she was really far more expert than I on what she had experienced and on what had helped her and what had not. She would need to decide which medication had been most helpful; if no medicine had been helpful in the slightest, then perhaps we should consider a course of no medication. After I took that position, she decided to take the Elavil consistently and reliably, which she continued to do over a substantial period of time.

It is a good idea for physicians to bear in mind that the higher the pedestal on which they let their patients place them, the farther they have to fall.

The prescription of medication is a special type of direct therapeutic intervention. A concrete offering is made to the patient in the hope that full patient compliance with that offering will help the patient to feel better. Patients' responses to medications are diagnostic in that they can help therapists predict how patients will respond to other direct interventions, verbal or otherwise. Do patients take the medication as prescribed? Do they refuse to take it? Do they modify directions? Do they have a penchant for severe side effects, abuse, or even overdosing on the medication? Do they feel better or worse?

If a patient's history is replete with medication failures, the therapist should consider employing paradox in the psychotherapy, since such interventions prove useful with patients who have difficulty taking in what others offer them and who are more skilled at rejecting, opposing, or ignoring that which is offered.

Case 5

Frederic, a 63-year-old man, was terrified of trying to walk again after he had received a prosthesis for an amputated leg. Every time he attempted to use a walker, he became paralyzed with fear. Prior to my seeing him, he had received Xanax, which he had taken regularly and as prescribed, with resulting temporary relief. He wanted to receive more definitive psycho-therapeutic assistance for his problem, however, so that he did not have to rely on the Xanax. His history of medication response was one of many features of his history and interactions with me that led me to devise a therapy that consisted primarily of direct intervention. For example, I had him increase the distance he traversed with his walker by one-half inch per day. If Frederic had episodes of panic, he agreed to awaken in the middle of the subsequent night in order to exercise—a therapeutic ordeal. He followed every directive to the letter and had no further feelings of terror.

Case 6

A 41-year-old woman, Claudia, had a history of chronic, severe tension headaches which had not been helped by innumerable medications. They either produced side effects or simply did not help. Other treatment, such as biofeedback, had also failed. The total ineffectiveness or counterproduc-tiveness of a wide array of medications for a condition that often responds to some medication suggested the potential usefulness of paradox. It appeared likely that Claudia would respond to direct psychotherapeutic intervention—homework tasks, empathic statements, clarifications, interpretations and directives—in the same fashion as she had to medications; that is, she would feel worse, or would ignore, reject, or oppose them. Indeed, an early assignment for her to keep a diary of her headaches was not performed. Her symptoms did respond, however, to a reframing of her headaches as helpful to her husband and a symptom prescription that her headaches continue.

Case 7

Steve was a 30-year-old man who had a long history of anxiety when eating with other people. The anxiety was so severe that it often caused him to feel nauseated or even to vomit and made it difficult for him to manipulate eating utensils because he shook so violently. Psychotropic medications had been previously prescribed twice by others. An antidepressant did not help, and a minor tranquilizer was not taken by the patient, who did not want to utilize such agents. Additional history revealed that Steve had terminated with a previous therapist after that therapist had directed him to keep a diary of his symptoms. He had refused to do this out of fear that a focus on his symptoms would worsen them. During my initial meeting with him, he appeared as an eager-to-please young man who agreed with everything I said. He became visibly anxious, however, when I asked him about his feelings toward or relationships with other people. These data suggested a discomfort with focusing on his own immediate emotional experiences. They also suggested an anxiety about taking in what others gave him if the offerings—verbal interventions, homework tasks, or medications—were too directly related to his symptoms. Nevertheless, he acted as if he were interested in pleasing and in being directed by another person.

For these reasons, the primary interventions in the therapy consisted of directives to perform tasks that were only indirectly related to his presenting problem. For example, he performed a homework assignment to travel alone to a local park to study how no two blades of grass are exactly the same in appearance. I also talked with him metaphorically about food, without any reference to his symptoms, discussing his likes and dislikes, how his food preferences were different from those of others, and how his tastes had changed during the process of growing up. Indirect hypnotic work was also done, in which he dealt with his problem by focusing on his breathing and the innate wisdom of his unconscious, which allowed him to take in just the right amount of oxygen comfortably and without regard for anything except his own physiological needs. These interventions eventually resulted in total resolution of Steve's symptoms.

Case 8

A final case illustrates several points. A 40-year-old man, Gene, had an eight-year history of marked depression and abdominal pain that had coincided in onset with the departure of his retired parents to the opposite end of the country. Medical workups for his pain had always been negative. He had been treated for these problems by numerous psychiatrists and several inpatient units. He had also received unsuccessful courses of treatment with an enormous number of psychotropic medications. Some of these medications produced no improvement. Other medications initially produced improvement over several weeks until they had to be discontinued either because the patient would complain vehemently of side effects or because of his belief that the medication was not helping him and needed to be changed. Gene had a history of frequently stopping treatment and of discontinuing medication. He had experienced a miserable childhood, filled with abuse and deprivation. Although his current life was one of unemployment, social isolation, and emptiness, he denied any problems besides his pain, which he felt was of a medical nature. He was not interested in psychotherapy. Despite his expressed dissatisfaction with all doctors, he conveyed no ideas about what he, himself, thought might be useful, leaving everything up to me. His response to my request for him to keep a daily diary of his symptoms was to do it for two days and then stop.

I felt that his history of rejecting and invalidating traditional, direct interventions suggested that paradox should be employed. I expressed concern that symptomatic relief would make him feel worse because there was nothing in his life to occupy his time and energy once he felt better. I predicted that, at some point in treatment, he would feel worse, become dissatisfied with me, and want to stop treatment for similar reasons.

I then prescribed one of the few existing antidepressants he had never received, protryptyline. He felt significantly better during the next three weeks. Even though there was still some pain, it was now tolerable. I then told him that it did not sound like the medicine had really helped him because he was still having pain, not to mention some minor, but unpleasant side effects. As a result, I stopped the protryptyline. During our next meeting, he bemoaned the fact that he was feeling worse, wondered when he would get the help he needed, but declined to state what he thought would be helpful. He left without a prescription. I told him that, because it was his body that was in pain and because *he* was the one who had to suffer the side effects of treatment, I was interested in doing only what *he* felt would be useful.

During the next visit, he angrily requested medication. I insisted that he select one because it was *his* pain and he had had much experience with medications. It was only then that he recalled that there had been an antidepressant, imipramine, that had once helped him, although his physician had switched to another medication for reasons unclear to him. With much annoyance at having to choose his own medication, he requested the imipramine, which I prescribed.

Over the next three months he felt much better and felt better for a longer period of time than he had for eight years. He was thinking seriously about getting a job and was becoming more socially active. During this time, I continued to utter dire warnings about the adverse consequences of his feeling too good. I continued to predict periodically that he might either stop the imipramine or terminate.

Although I believe this case illustrates a useful role for strategic interventions in the prescription of medication, its ending is not satisfactory. The patient angrily terminated treatment after I returned from a month-long vacation. At our last session, he stated I had not helped him at all, despite that fact that he was still feeling markedly better.

In this case, I employed a series of paradoxical interventions. I took a devil's advocate position, in which I cautioned against pain relief and predicted failure. Roles also became reversed: Instead of *his* stopping the protryptyline because it was not helping when it actually was, *I* stopped it with an explanation that it was not helping him when it actually appeared to be. Because I took that role, he was obligated to assume the complementary role of an individual who wanted medication to be prescribed. This was a role that previously had been assumed only by his physicians. In interpersonal systems, it is more important that certain roles are filled than who it is that fills them. If the therapist of an ambivalent patient takes one side, the patient may be obligated to take the other.

A corollary of the role reversal was my one-down positioning with respect to the prescription of medication. I assumed a position of deference to his better judgment and passive compliance with his request. This was essentially the stance *he* had taken with all previous physicians: a passive compliance by a "dumb" patient with whatever they foisted upon him, only to be followed by a rejection and/or disqualification of what they had offered.

My withholding and discontinuation of medication that was potentially or actually helpful initially created a therapeutic relationship based on deprivation. His history indicated that he was more familiar and less anxious with relationships characterized by this quality than with relationships based upon his being nurtured. Indeed, he became engaged in therapy and kept his appointments meticulously until I (presumably) "abandoned" him by going on vacation, much as his parents had done eight years before at the onset of his symptoms.

The prescribing and the taking of medication are patterns of behavior that are influenced by the interpersonal context in which they occur. Just as with the administration of therapeutic advice, psychoanalytic interpretations, desensitizing hierarchies, or elegant paradoxical prescriptions, the way the therapist gives help has much to do with whether another individual will decide whether to accept what is offered. Several cases which relied upon the use of indirect approaches have been cited to illustrate the usefulness of Ericksonian approaches for administering medication to potentially difficult patients.

Ericksonian Hypnosis and Psychotherapy in Clinical Settings

Juliet Auer, C.Q.S.W., M. Phil.

Juliet Auer, C.Q.S.W. (Oxford Polytechnic), M. Phil. (Southampton) is a social worker and psychosexual counselor at the Renal Unit of Churchill Hospital in Oxford, UK, and a Junior Fellow at the University of Southampton. She has served as Chair of the British Association of Social Work, Nephrology Group, and is a Founding Member of the London Society for Ericksonian Psychotherapy and Hypnosis. She has published on the psychosocial aspects of dialysis.

Conducting effective therapy in the Renal Unit of a large hospital is a difficult task. In this setting Auer has found it beneficial to use Ericksonian methods. She presents three cases to document her approach.

The differences between outpatient sessions in the therapist's consulting rooms and therapy conducted at the bedside of inpatients in crisis are extreme. The former can be likened to a planned procedure in a well-prepared and equipped operating theatre. The surroundings and context have been designed for a specific purpose. The latter is like the task of the army field surgeon, operating under fire with minimal facilities, no control over the environment, and relying heavily on the creative use of anything that comes to hand. One is working "where the patient is," not only in the psychological sense, but physically. Patients may be attached to life support machinery, lying in a noisy public ward, or undergoing painful or frightening procedures. There is seldom opportunity for extensive history taking, and even less chance for detailed planning of an intervention. The situation is usually noisy, lacking in privacy, and far removed from the conventional comforts of therapy. In this setting, therapy is a matter of thinking on one's feet, often literally, since even a chair is inappropriate when working with a patient who is undergoing a kidney biopsy or surgery to create access for a dialysis machine. In the setting of a large

Address reprint requests to Juliet Auer, C.Q.S.W., Wychwood 23, Church Green Witney, Oxon, OX8 6A2 England.

hospital renal unit, I have found that one of the most effective frameworks for intervention is Ericksonian hypnotherapy.

The lack of the quiet, controllable environment of the consulting room, with some degree of predictability, has proven to be a benefit rather than a disadvantage. Therapists working in a hospital have inside knowledge of the system and situation that is "part of the problem," and are, thus, able to create small changes in dynamics from within rather than from without. Perhaps the simplest example of this technique is "Reframing the doctor," subtitled "What every good hostess knows." Patients with renal failure feel helpless, with no control over their illness or treatments. They are often in awe of the doctor, and afraid to ask questions. My therapeutic aim is generally to help patients feel confident and assertive enough to address questions and discuss options with the doctor. Another objective is to access resources which enable them to exercise influence over their condition and make a positive contribution to treatment. Working outside the setting, one might well achieve this desired outcome, but not without considerable investment of time and the cooperation of the patient.

The insider's solution is often faster and less complicated. Working in a team, I know my colleagues' interests. When a doctor and a patient are together, I introduce a nonmedical topic that I know the doctor cannot resist, and the patient can discuss with confidence and, preferably, superior knowledge. In this way, a bridge is created. I have introduced topics such as carpentry, the merits of Japanese cars, Irish ancestry, football, gardening, computers and dog training. The resulting conversation not only breaks the ice and shifts the context, but elicits such remarks from the patient as: "Isn't he a nice man, not at all like a doctor." Once patients see the physician as a person, and one with whom they have something in common, they can start to tackle the illness together. This is a simple cocktail party strategy that deserves to be moved to the clinic, the ward, and even the operating theatre.

Example number two I call "The ward round game." The ward round is a ritual of almost mystical significance in the teaching hospital. Senior physician and retinue visit each bed in turn, and discuss patients, as if they were not present. Their chosen language is jargon, and it almost seems specifically designed to raise patients' anxiety levels. There is seldom any eye contact with patients. Perhaps, if there were, doctors would not fail to observe signs such as sweating and panic. Having discussed the patient with colleagues and students, the doctor suddenly changes his or her tone of voice, appearing to notice the patient for the first time. "You're doing all right. There's nothing to worry about. No questions? Good."

My self-prescribed task is to observe the patient's face throughout the ordeal, noting the words and omissions that have caused greatest stress.

However unaware the doctor may be of the nonverbal reactions, the patient is generally supersensitive to every glance, tone, and expression exchanged between the experts.

> I don't like the look of the AF on this ECG. No MI on enzymes, but longstanding malignant hypertension. Pyrexial, too, uh-huh (significant look). Have we looked for vegetation? Do you think we're missing SBE? Perhaps we ought to. Hm (knowing nod).

As they move to the next bed, I try to mop up the worst of the psychological damage:

> No, malignant doesn't mean cancer—and they've proved you didn't have a heart attack. They want to find out why you still have a temperature. No, vegetation isn't plant life, just germs. They make it sound like the "Day of the Triffids," don't they? If you want to know more, I'll get the doctor to come and explain later.

Once I learned observational skills, particularly those of nonverbal cuing, it became easy to tell which patients needed more information, how full or detailed the information needed to be, and, of course, which patients did not want to know. As one can see, these general activities on the ward afford many challenges and opportunities for working along Ericksonian lines. Some case examples will show more specific uses of my observations and the applications of tailored interventions.

An Ericksonian approach is ideally suited to therapy in the hospital because it relies on the discovery of innate resources. The use of imagination during light or deep trance states can broaden the horizons of a patient who is severely limited physically. The ability to explore an inner world whose limits are unconfined can create a sense of mastery that can help to abate the unpleasant external reality. Erickson's use of this method with terminally ill patients is described by Haley (1973).

The concept of reframing has proven very useful with patients who dread the approaching need for dialysis. In spite of its life-sustaining effect, the machine represents a threat to the patient's autonomy. It is seen as a relentless taskmaster, demanding, "Your time or your life." It is also a constant and concrete reminder that the patient is no longer viable without artificial life support. While the diabetic is equally dependent upon insulin replacement, there is no real comparison to the dialysis machine in terms of the time involved in treatment or the sense of external versus internal control. I have found that it is necessary to reframe the helping aspect of the machine by shifting the image from a dominating tyrant to an obedient servant which can serve its master, the patient. The time involved in treatment, usually seem as "time lost," can be perceived as a creative and valuable period, as some case examples will show.

The Case of M

M, in his mid-forties, was a minister of a busy parish. The diagnosis of renal failure, needing imminent dialysis, came as a complete shock to him. It signified the end of everything, since he could not believe that he would be able to continue his parish work as a dialysis patient. He reacted in the context of his faith and experienced a sense of unjust punishment meted out by the God he was trying to serve. In a crisis of faith, he was deeply depressed. When I saw him on the ward he had little idea of what dialysis was really like, and he was anticipating pain.

Dialysis involves inserting large hollow needles into the arm veins. This procedure is, in fact, made painless by the use of local anesthesia. It is fruitless to tell a patient, "It will not hurt," many associate that particular phrase to early visits to the dentist or mothers washing the grazed knee with iodine.

During our first conversation M expressed numerous anxieties. He felt a burden to his colleagues who were covering his work; he worried he would not be able to support his frail and anxious wife; he could not accept needing help when he had always been the one to give help. Finally, he "confessed" that he felt suicidal, which was a betrayal of his faith. His wife had told him that it was blasphemous to talk of suicide, further compounding his guilt. This seemed to be the most sensitive spot. So, rather than feeding his sense of shame by treating it as an issue, I asked, "Do you really think that being a priest should stop you feeling like any other human being?" This rhetorical question invited no further discussion. It also suggested that his reaction was not unusual. I then approached the practical matter of dialysis.

> I'm not surprised you're dreading dialysis. In your place I would be dreading it, too. I've seen so many people go through this experience, and those 15 hours a week can be terrible. Dialysis is so excruciatingly... boring.

The adjective was, as I had hoped, the last one he was expecting, and had the effect of stunning him into a sudden reassessment of the situation. He had been listening to a familiar story with a known ending. Suddenly the denouement was quite different. This format used pacing, to engage the patient and create rapport, followed by a confusional shift at a critical moment.

The best evidence for the hypnotic effect of this sort of communication is the silence that follows, while the facial expressions reveal an internal search, trying to reconcile the new data with the preconception. Boring equals grey, uneventful, lacking in stimuli, but dialysis equals red (with blood,) sharp (with needles), anxious (with life or death involved). After a long pause:

Th: After all, what are you going to do with all that spare time?

M: (tentatively) I suppose one hand will be free. Can one write letters?

Th: Yes, but who wants to write letters for 15 hours a week?

M: But if I can write letters, I could do other parish paperwork.

Th: I suppose so, but how many hours paperwork do you do in a week?

M: Well, with sermons to write as well, I should think it must be about 10 hours a week.

Th: You still have five hours doing nothing, that's a long time.

M: Can one make phone calls on the machine?

Th: Of course, we always install a phone beside the machine for dialysis at home.

M: I do a lot of parish work on the phone.

Th: Five hours of it?

M: I should think it adds up to about three. Then, of course I have to do a lot of reading...

The benefit of this method is self-evident. Once a patient begins to focus on the task of filling time during dialysis, ideas that follow are self-generated and congruent. If therapists make suggestions, patients typically find objections. Given the freedom to explore his own resources, M lost all unreasonable fear of dialysis, never mentioned suicide again, and realized that he did not have to give up his parish. This technique is a variation of reframing, in which patients' versions of a situation are not redefined by the therapist, but are apparently confirmed, only to be suddenly obliterated. Patients are then encouraged to reconstruct a different picture within an empty frame.

In my experience, many fears of treatment are rational, even if misguided due to ignorance. When a patient does struggle with irrational fear, it is helpful to try a different approach, one based on the patient's model of the world.

The Case of R

R, who was offered a transplant, told me he had a premonition that he would die as a result of the operation. The operation was successful and the early postoperative course uncomplicated. R still assured me, however, that he knew he was going to die. No amount of reason can help the patient with a "premonition" because such feelings are not rational. After a few days he developed a chest infection and steadily declined over two weeks to the point when the doctors considered his life to be in the balance. His own view was resigned, but the message was basically, "I told you so." In this extreme situation, I was prepared to break my general rule of being totally honest with patients. I therefore told him that during the previous night, I had suddenly had the conviction that all was going to be well with him, and that he would survive. I did not *think* this was the case, I *knew* it.

It was now a battle as to whose belief was the stronger or more valid. R could no more argue with my unreason than I could with his. I felt it necessary to set a time limit on the contest, so asked him to say how long it would be before we knew who was right. He replied that if he survived the next 24 hours, he would accept that I had "won." His condition remained critical but stable over that period, after which he began to improve. There were no further setbacks. This is a case of meeting the client at his model of the world no matter how extreme (Lankton & Lankton, 1983). Faced with an irrational problem, one may need an irrational solution.

The Case of B

The next case deals with a patient who had already started dialysis. B was referred because of panic attacks, both before and during dialysis, and restlessness due to discomfort. She had a plasmacytoma of the sacrum, which made it particularly painful to lie still during a four to five hour period on the machine.

It was agreed that I would give her relaxation training to help reduce discomfort. Treatment took place while B was in bed on a busy ward. After a standard session, in which she was learning to check each set of muscles for tension, B was less anxious. She thought that the session was over. I then asked her if there was any particular music she liked, because she might find relaxation easier if she listened to music on a personal stereo during dialysis. She replied that her favorite was Mozart, and that she liked the opera more than any other music. This provided the opportunity to use trance:

Th: Do you remember the last time you went to the opera?
B: Yes, very well.
Th: Have you noticed that after a great performance, there is sometimes a moment of silence before the applause starts. It's as if the audience

has been transported into another world, and it takes a few moments for them to come back into themselves.

B: Yes, I find that happens with me.

Th: And it's a good experience. There is something magical about the opera, the exciting smells and sounds in the auditorium, the expectant hush as the lights dim and the conductor appears (B's eyes closed). Then the overture starts. I expect you can almost hear the music. (B nods) You can go on listening as long as you want, because there is no need to be aware of any sounds except the ones you want to hear. You need not even listen to my voice, but you may be surprised to realize that you can go to the opera any time you want. You can enter that magical world in which nothing matters but the story and the beauty of the music. Perhaps you can notice with part of your mind that in that other world, you cease to be aware of yourself at all. You no longer feel the seat, and you do not want to move. Your body hardly seems to belong to you because your senses are numbed to everything but the sights and sounds of the story, and you can go on listening as long as you want. When the music is over, you will come back into your body, and you will feel good. You will open your eyes and you will feel comfortable and peaceful.

I returned after 20 minutes. B was lying restfully with a smile on her face.

Th: Which opera have you been to ?

B: "The Magic Flute." (possibly influenced by my use of "magical")

Th: It is good to know you can go whenever you want to. Why don't you go again tomorrow instead of going on dialysis?

The next day I brought in a personal stereo and a tape of "The Magic Flute." One hour before she was due to go on treatment, when she would normally have been getting very anxious, I gave her the headset, started the music, and repeated the induction of the previous day. On this occasion my voice could only be heard distantly as a background to the music. She later listened throughout her dialysis session without further induction. According to the nurses, she was not demanding, restless, or anxious. B "attended" many operas over the next few months. Her husband, who had previously been inclined to withdraw from the situation because he was so exasperated with his inability to help her, bought a stereo and a quantity of tapes. She later transferred to a unit nearer her home. When I saw her about a year later, she was attending an outpatient clinic with her husband. Both looked well and happy. B called me over to speak. "I just wanted to thank you," she said. "It's a strange thing, but that music made all the difference."

It was, of course, extremely lucky that she chose opera. It is difficult to concoct any other occasion in which one may sit almost motionless on a cramped seat for four hours on end, so entranced that one is unaware of discomfort or unrelated external stimuli.

To the patients, the worst thing about chronic illness is the sense of powerlessness and loss of control over events. The next case shows that in spite of feelings of extreme helplessness, a careful intervention can create the option of control and empowerment.

The Case of P

P was a transplant patient in his late twenties. He had been adopted as a baby and had a strong sense of not "belonging" in his adoptive family. He was mild mannered, intelligent, ambitious, well read, and felt little in common with his kindly, concerned, but simple parents. He also felt suffocated by their concern and was eager to leave home and become independent. He had shown great determination both as a dialysis patient and after his transplant. He had taken a degree, written a doctoral thesis, and competed regularly in the International Transplant Games.

P was admitted to the hospital with a persistent febrile illness, diarrhea, weight loss and weakness. He was found to have bone marrow suppression, leading to a dangerously low white blood cell count, and failure of immune responses. The illness had many features of AIDS but was negative to this and all other viral tests. His immunosuppression to prevent kidney rejection was stopped, but over the next two weeks his white cell count continued to fall. Medical staff were baffled, and could do no more than wait and hope that his white cell count would rise before an opportunistic infection proved fatal.

When I saw P, he was bedridden with a high fever. He was too weak to stand. His state of near delirium was ideally suited to hypnotic methods of communication, because he was already in a region halfway between reality and a dream state. I asked if he believed in the power of mind over matter. He replied that he did, and that his belief was very strong. Knowing his determination, it seemed likely that he imposed conscious willpower to attempt solutions; however, in his present condition, he needed to allow unconscious resources from within to fight the battle for him.

I said that if he was interested in the way the mind could help the body, he would probably find nothing surprising in a true story that I would tell him. I related a case of a colleague, in which he had treated a child with a similar condition by getting him to picture his white cells as the "goodies," and the invading germs as the cowardly "baddies." The child was told to encourage the goodies, to imagine them rallying to his defense and multiplying. He drew pictures of them fighting the invaders. He mentally called up his defenses and cheered them on. The outcome had been successful. I pointed out that this had been treatment for a child, but that P could find himself knowing how to use these resources of the unconscious mind in the way that suited him.

An advantage of this situation was that P was effectively bound to identify with the child because he was in such a helpless condition. This was reinforced by the context of listening to a story at the bedside recalling childhood. The drawback was that his conscious mind was fighting for control of his situation, and especially for independence and freedom from his parents.

A few days passed with only marginal improvement in his immune defenses. The next time I visited P, he was in an agony of frustration at his helplessness. He felt too weak to do anything for himself and expressed great frustration over the fact that he had been visited by his adoptive father, even though he had expressly told the nurses he did not want to see his parents. He did not feel able to make the request again, since this seemed to be the final proof of his inability to control events around him. P's overriding need seemed to be proof, however small, that he could influence events. Therefore, I told him I could show him beyond doubt that he still had power. P protested weakly that this was impossible.

Th: When you want me to leave, you have only to say "Please go now" and I will leave. You have power over me.
P: But I don't mind you visiting.
Th: Nevertheless, there will be a moment when you have had enough and want me to go. All you have to do is dismiss me when you wish.

P was a mild mannered and polite young man, not given to dismissing anyone. I sat down. He was still very feverish, with a low white cell count. He drifted in and out of trance states as I quietly talked about the ways in which his unconscious mind could help him with his problem. There were long but not uncomfortable silences. Half an hour passed, three quarters, then an hour. It was well after my time for going home, but I was not going to leave until P had exercised his power over me. Finally, he turned his head, smiled and said, "Would you please go now."

This situation could not fail to have a successful outcome from P's point of view. Having defined myself as in his power, I would have had to ask for his permission to leave, if he had not dismissed me within the next hour or so. Either way, he was in charge.

Two days later his temperature was down, and his white cell count had risen to a near normal level. The doctors confirmed that there was no medical explanation for his dramatic recovery. Two weeks later, P had resumed jogging. When seen in outpatient clinic, he said that it had just been a question of mind over matter.

No one will ever know whether that intervention made a clinical difference, but the change in P's morale was evident. The episode also taught me that an Ericksonian therapist need never be empty-handed. When we have nothing else in the environment that can be used to promote change, we can redefine ourselves, which automatically shifts the position of the patient.

Conclusion

In the hospital setting, encounters with the patient may be brief and unstructured. By adopting Ericksonian principles these encounters, even a greeting in a corridor can become an opportunity for creative work. By putting these principles into action, one can adopt new, although at times unnerving, ways of looking at situations, people and interactions. As these cases illustrate, one cannot be a part-time Ericksonian. The opportunities are everywhere.

References

Haley, J. (1973). *Uncommon therapy: The psychiatric approach of Milton H. Erickson, M.D.* New York: Norton.
Lankton, S. & Lankton, C. (1983). *The answer within: A clinical framework of Ericksonian hypnotherapy.* New York: Brunner/Mazel.

Ten-Minute Trance: Ericksonian Techniques in a Busy General Medical Practice

Bob Britchford, MRCPsych.

Bob Britchford, LRCP, MRCS, MRCPsych (Westminster Medical School, London, England) is a General Practitioner and Consultant Child Psychiatrist in Swindon, Wiltshire, England.

Britchford explains how he began to use and adapt Ericksonian techniques in a busy family medicine practice. Although his setting did not allow for extended treatment hours, he was able to accommodate with what he calls "the ten-minute trance."

Family practitioners have a busy and exacting life with many patients who have a wide assortment of problems. Although their training is medical and scientific, many of the problems family practitioners deal with are psychological, or have psychological overtones. In a way, they are explorers in the area of psychological problems. Explorers in varied landscapes need to be navigators, leaders, negotiators, diplomats, mountaineers and fountains of wisdom. Because of the "terrain" in which they work, family doctors need equally varied skills. They find themselves able to use some of the skills of psychologists, counselors, priests, elders, salesmen, and even soothsayers.

Erickson, with his chimera-like aspect, difficult to define and ever different, seems to be an ideal model for family medicine. This chapter describes my efforts to apply Ericksonian approaches in family medicine, and provides a critique of the resulting experiences over the last three years of work.

In my practice it is a fact of life that I have to see a patient about every ten minutes. This is not inflexible and some patients take longer than others. The ten-minute consultation is an average. Some days I see 30 patients and

Address reprint requests to Bob Britchford, MRCPsych., River House, Goose Green, Lambourn, Berkshire, England RG16 7YB.

some days 50. Patients attend as they see fit, as it is a free service. The number coming each day varies according to the season and illness trends and is, therefore, unpredictable.

When I discovered the work of Erickson, I was very excited but also confused by the complexity and subtlety of his work. I threw myself into the study of Ericksonian methods and began applying them wherever and whenever I could, including in my own family. I began applying several techniques very quickly, and the techniques seemed to click into place in general medical practice. It was like hailing an old friend I had never met.

My first application of Ericksonian methods in the very short medical consultation was to do the passive things first. I concentrated on the observation of nonverbal behavior and minimal signs. I also tried to practice one technique at a time. I would spend a week practicing pacing verbally, a week pacing nonverbally, a week concentrating on simple metaphors, another on delivery of interventions, and so on. Trying to separate things in this way enabled me to become more comfortable in my newfound confusion. As soon as my rawness with Ericksonian methods passed, I was able to relax and apply techniques as and when they felt appropriate.

Ericksonian Techniques in the Short Interview

I, thus, come to what I have been doing for the last three years. Dealing with patients in an average time of ten minutes is difficult. It is extremely easy to get behind. In this setting one has to accept that there will be times when everything seems to happen at once. The recently bereaved widow comes just after the child has been sick on the carpet and just before the girl who is not sure she wants an abortion. In order to better illustrate how to work in this setting, I will describe a typical consultation, then discuss some advantages and disadvantages of my approach.

Preparation

I begin a consultation by reminding myself who the patient is, who is in their family that I also know, the last time the patient was seen, and why. Next, I call the patient personally from the waiting room and begin observing the patient getting up and coming in. Many doctors whose offices I have visited call the next patient by intercom, or just a buzzer or bell, to save them "wasting time" getting out of their chair. I'm not sure why, but I have come to vary the way I call the patient. I will sometimes walk jauntily, sometimes idly, sometimes briskly. Perhaps somewhat fancifully, I believe that this can set the tone or the mood of the coming consultation.

I know the majority of my patients and the themes of my relationship from previous encounters, and have clearly established in my mind who the patient is, I have some idea what tone I might want to set. I observe carefully the way patients walk in. They might be businesslike, apologetic, sly, careful. They may look ill or in pain. I observe carefully. The more I observe, the more I find myself seeing.

Choice of Words and Emphasis

I choose my words carefully. "How can I help you?" "How are you getting on?" "How are your feeling?" "What can I do for you?" These are very different opening questions. This is similar to Wilk (1983), who used to set tasks for clients and, at the follow-up interview, instead of asking as his very first question, "How are you?" he would more usually say something like, "Well, what did you do and how did it go?"

Often patients begin with an elaborate set of symptoms and a labyrinth of details, and my reply might be equally woven. "What did you have in mind I might do for you about this?" I try to match the opening questions to patients' faces and the way they present themselves that day. "What is your *main* worry in all of this?" might be a way of questioning someone who is straightforward and pragmatic in their outlook, but who has presented a long list of symptoms from which to choose.

I would rarely ask, "How do you connect all of these things?" I might ask, "How had you thought I might connect all of these things?" More likely I would not want them to make associations at all. This careful choice of words, which takes practice and concentration, is something that I do throughout the length of the interview and is not just confined to the opening remarks.

I listen throughout to the patient's emphasis. This is usually nonverbal—a tone, a leaning forward, a pained look. The patient's emphasis is often quite subtle, perhaps a change in muscle tone in the face, or a slight shifting in the seat. Observing such behavior is no more difficult than merely being attuned to the possibility that such subtlety exists. This practice is similar to observing trance phenomena in hypnotic work. Having noted the various emphases, I make sure to deal with them before the consultation ends.

I observe exact parts of the body which the patient points to as they describe their symptoms. If someone describes a chest pain just to the right of the sternum in the fifth rib interspace, I make sure to include that exact point in my examination. It is usually the first or, emphatically, the last place I put my stethoscope. I listen to the precise words used to describe the symptoms, and often use those exact words back when discussing the symptom or when summing up. If a patient says a pain "gets" him or "grips" him, I use "get" and "grip" when pronouncing on that symptom. Similarly, if a patient wants to describe something as "phlegm" or "catarrh" or "bile" I use these same words back. This sounds obvious but it is surprisingly easy to change the patient's word into the medical word for the same thing. The patient calls it "phlegm" and the doctors refer to it as "sputum."

Throughout my initial contact, I am formulating my questions in such a way as to lead the patient away from negative associations and toward therapeutic ones. If someone says, perhaps casually, perhaps with meaning, "I have been like this ever since my mother went into the hospital," I note the association. I may choose to loosen it and I may choose to do it immediately or to postpone it. I may bring it into the open: "Have you been leading yourself to suppose that your mother going into the hospital might have something to do with this?" Before long, initial planning has been formulated and observations have been mentally recorded. I then involve myself fully with examinations.

Examinations

When carrying out examinations, trance techniques are extremely useful. By talking about the symptoms or telling stories, or using suspense or distraction, patients can be led to relaxing so much that they are only marginally aware of the examination taking place. Children are particularly susceptible to this and the younger they are the more susceptible. Young babies will fix their eyes on one's face or on slow movements. Touching their front while examining their back is an example of giving them a prominent, interesting and nice experience to occupy them while the necessary examination is taking place out of their awareness (behind their back—literally, in this case). I used to find it quite difficult to examine a patient's abdomen without the patient tensing up. I now, almost without exception, use some distracting or confusing technique during abdominal examinations, and I no longer have much difficulty doing them. Once again, this is easiest with children, who seem to concentrate very hard on my questions or my pantomime type behavior to the exclusion of their worries about the examination.

When commenting during an examination, I take account of patients' whole views of themselves. I recently treated a young man, a minor pop-singer, who was something of a hunk with well-proportioned muscle development. He had several complaints, but his main one was of pain and restriction in his shoulder movements. As I was completing my examination I said the following, "With regard to the long-term outlook here (pause) I would reckon that a *young* chap like you (pause) a *strong* chap as you are (pause) with *strong* muscles is not likely to have this pain for very long." This might sound rather cumbersome but is no longer in the saying than anything else a doctor might say when summarizing findings. The difference is in the choice of words and the choice of emphasis and pauses. One has to say something and one might as well say things in such a way as to influence the patients' view of themselves, provided that it is a true view and is congruent with the actual findings in the examination.

Similarly, when pronouncing on the result of a vaginal examination of a woman who is very keen on her appearance, figure, vigor and youth, I might choose the words "young-feeling" to describe her uterus. If the patient's main concern was her health, I might say "healthy" about her womb. I want to give patients an optimistic view of their body and one which is in tune with their main concerns. It is needless to repeat, I'm sure, that I am not giving a false view. I wouldn't say "healthy" if it were unhealthy, and so on.

The Context of Practice

Since studying Erickson, I have found that I wanted to influence not only my own practice but that of our staff. Our practice nurse, Geraldine, used to have the habit of calling me on the phone, with the patient sitting behind her, and saying, "Do you want to see Mrs. So-and-so today?" If, after discussing the problem, I said, "No," Mrs. So-and-so might feel unwanted. (Mrs. So-and-so listens to the words, "Do you want to see..."—answer, "No.") Another example was when Geraldine was helping me prepare to give an injection into a patient's knee. She asked me, "Do you want to use the big needle or the really big one?" I have since taught Geraldine to pick her words more carefully!

During the last three years, I have become more conscious of the whole context in which I work. Too many hospitals and doctors' offices in my experience have markers, context markers as they have been called (Wilk & O'Hanlon, 1987), which set the mood of discomfort and anxiety: Nurses in white uniforms, brisk and off-hand receptionists, dismembered voices from intercoms, clinical smells. In the family practitioner setting, most of these are unnecessary. Having become more conscious of using anything to aid my patients' sense of comfort and well-being, I have realized that the first part of trance induction for my patients is when they enter the building in which I work. By eliminating bossy health education posters, buzzers, bells, and other signs of impersonal medicine, and keeping the stigma of the operating theatre to a minimum, I feel I contribute to a sense of being at home rather than being in a threatening environment. To many of his visitors, Erickson was remarkable in the way he had his practice in his own home, surrounded by his family and numerous homely objects and props. Reading and hearing about the way Erickson conducted his practice has rubbed off on me.

Asides and Indirect Communication

When one overhears patients talking to each other about what their doctor said to them, they often seem to have been struck by one remark or another. The thing that struck them or that they remember is often a chance remark or joke or an aside. When using hypnotic or focused communication techniques, it is possible to make chance remarks more telling.

I was dealing with an 11-year-old girl, once, who was soiling herself. There seemed to be some issue around growing up. I wondered if soiling was proving that she was still a child. I accepted the girl's story that she could not help the soiling and gave her some squeezing exercises to do to build up the muscles around her bottom. As an aside to her mother, delivered in an adult, knowing way, I said, "Of course, her periods are going to start soon and that will make her pants dirty. She doesn't want to have two reasons for them to be dirty, does she?" The girl's soiling stopped and her mother started allowing her more freedom and responsibility. There is no way of knowing, but it seemed to me that the aside about her period was an essential part of the success.

When giving injections or doing other potentially painful procedures, I have sometimes, though by no means always, been able to help the patient achieve freedom from pain or anxiety. I never use the word "hypnosis" and rarely use formal inductions. I tell a story to the nurse, using the drama of the story or the rhythms of my speech to induce an altered state in the patient. I make it clear to the patient that this is casual and natural. Since this "treatment" is not being offered to patients directly, they have no opportunity to refuse it.

Negotiating a Conclusion

I try to knead or coax the consultation to a satisfying conclusion. A patient in my setting expects a short consultation and so time is not necessarily a hindrance here. Even so, one can make the interview seem timeless by paying very close attention to the problem. Time, in hypnosis, can seem infinitely malleable and I try to take advantage of this.

Because I see many patients more than once for any given problem and, in fact, treat the majority of patients on a life-long basis, each visit can be seen as part of an extended treatment. Because many of the circumstances are the same on each occasion—the patient and I are the same people, the office is the same, the lighting, the chair, the sounds, etc.—it can be thought that the patient is able to enter the same state of consciousness or trance that they were last in when sitting in that same chair. Viewed in this way, it is possible to undertake more extended and complex work than an average time of ten minutes would be thought to allow.

The conclusion of a consultation comes ideally when both doctor and patient are satisfied with that moment and that way to end it. This does not always happen. Patients who haven't studied nonverbal behavior fail to observe that I am ready to see them go!

Often, I am thinking about the end of a consultation from the time it starts. The technique is borrowed and modified from O'Hanlon and Wilk's (1987) ideas on negotiating the presenting complaint. If I see a difficulty arising in the early part of the consultation—perhaps a large gap between the way I view the problem and the way the patient views it—I may start seeding ideas or moulding the interchange in such a way that the patient and I can arrive at a mutually satisfactory outcome in the time available. This may mean offering a treatment as an experiment or arranging some biological or behavioral test which will act as a starting point for some future consultation.

Problems

I have shown how I have implemented Ericksonian techniques in family practice medicine. I use them and I will continue to do so, refining the techniques as I go. While I am convinced that family practitioners every-where could find these methods useful and engaging, there have been drawbacks.

Rosen (1983) told the following story, which describes a videotape Erickson made while working with Ernest Rossi and others:

> Erickson was hypnotizing me and a few other people, and at one point he stopped and he asked Ernie, "Do I look very tense?" And of course nobody thought Erickson could be tense. Ernie said, "No. Do you feel tense?" And he said, "Yes, I do. I have to watch every movement I make. And I have to watch everything I do or say so that it will not interfere with the work of my patients."

I'm sure that anyone who has performed hypnosis will recognize the tension that Erickson was feeling. Practicing hypnosis is a concentrated exercise. The therapy can be very active, demanding and tiring. When mixing the demands of hypnosis with the practice of physical medicine, as I have done in the last three years, it has produced some headaches and some worries.

The headaches I refer to have been literal ones. After seeing 25 patients in a morning, practicing medicine, while also concentrating on observing them and refining my communications to them, I have often finished a day with a headache. The pressure of dealing with patients every ten minutes is great enough, in any event, but when this includes new skills to practice and learn, the pressure has been immense.

Developing any skill is hard work and the apprenticeship is the hardest phase. Having done my apprenticeship in medicine in the usual way, ten years later I found myself undergoing another apprenticeship, this time in Ericksonian techniques. At one point I was so often tense I thought I would abandon my application of Ericksonian techniques. I tried, once, and was confounded to find that I could not do it. Having trained myself to observe, I could not stop observing. I continued to see all the nonverbal behaviors which I hadn't been seeing before. This is something of a warning to someone thinking of taking up these techniques. Like any skill, it is difficult to unlearn.

A recurring worry I have had is whether the quality of my medical judgments and my medical treatments has suffered as a result of my concentration on Ericksonian techniques. I was talking to a widow who I saw frequently, and as I was listening to her recollections about her late husband, looking at her posture, small movements, skin color, etc., I wondered to myself whether I could also have room in my brain to be attuned to possible medical diagnoses. She was wistfully remembering times with her husband, and I realized that this was a practiced set of memories she was retelling and that her memories were always associated with a feeling of regret, sadness and loss, and that she exhibited many of the physiological signs of trance. If I were to influence the way she was going to be now, and in her future, I was going to have to alter her mood while she was indulging in these memories. I wanted to break into her story, using her own words, not to break the trance but to reframe some of these memories.

All very fine and clever. But this all took place in a few minutes. All my thinking time had been devoted to developing strategies to turn her into a happy widow. And I forgot to take her blood pressure, which was why she came. In her case it was not important because I see her regularly and was able to take the blood pressure the next time I saw her (and as I think more about her case, I realize that her blood pressure is only the ostensible reason she comes to see me).

Although I have not entirely resolved the worry about mixing Ericksonian and hypnotic techniques with medical practice, I find that the former fit so well with the latter that there has never been a clash of priorities. Medical "alarm bells" still ring louder and earlier than others, and I think that there is an unconscious mechanism at work which will ensure that this will continue to happen.

There is a final problem for doctors working under pressure who indulge in focused communication. That is, one sees problems more clearly; however, one has no more time to deal with them. One is able to read the sign but one does not have time to follow the tracks. Patients will give clues and cues, minimal or obvious, but I often have to stifle my desire to follow-up on them. A gynecologist told me that more than half the women he sees in a clinic give him hints that they are not satisfied with their sex lives. He said that if he took up any of these cues he would be overwhelmed with therapeutic consultation sessions. Apart from the most severe complaints, which he refers to a sexual counselor, he consciously decided to ignore the cues or deflect them. I know his problem but I don't know the answer.

Summary

Ericksonian approaches are appropriate skills to use in family practice. This chapter puts forward some ideas about the use of Ericksonian psychotherapy in family practice and describes experiences in implementing these successfully in a very limited time frame. Although physicians may experience several problems, including general confusion, occasional distraction, and fatigue, the effectiveness and reliability of this approach warrant its continued study and practice.

References

Rosen, S. (1983). *Ericksonian hypnotherapy simplified* (audiotape). Phoenix: The Milton H. Erickson Foundation.
Wilk, J. (1983). Personal communication.
Wilk, J., & O'Hanlon, B. (1987). *Shifting contexts*. New York: Guilford.